Heart Disease

FOR

DUMMIES®

POCKET EDITION

by James M. Rippe, MD

Look for Pocket Editions on these other topics:

Allergies For Dummies, Pocket Edition
Anxiety & Depression For Dummies, Pocket Edition
Asthma For Dummies, Pocket Edition
Diabetes For Dummies, Pocket Edition
Dieting For Dummies, Pocket Edition
High Blood Pressure For Dummies, Pocket Edition
Menopause For Dummies, Pocket Edition
Migraines For Dummies, Pocket Edition

WILEY

Wiley Publishing, Inc.

Heart Disease For Dummies,® Pocket Edition

Published by
Wiley Publishing, Inc.
111 River St.
Hoboken, NJ 07030-5774
www.wiley.com

Copyright © 2006 by Wiley Publishing, Inc., Indianapolis, Indiana

Published by Wiley Publishing, Inc., Indianapolis, Indiana

For general information on our other products and services, please contact our Customer Care Department within the U.S. at 800-762-2974, outside the U.S. at 317-572-3993, or fax 317-572-4002.

For technical support, please visit www.wiley.com/techsupport.

Wiley also publishes its books in a variety of electronic formats. Some content that appears in print may not be available in electronic books.

Library of Congress Control Number: 2005936644

ISBN-13: 978-0-471-79237-6

ISBN-10: 0-471-79237-3

Manufactured in the United States of America

10 9 8 7 6 5 4 3 2

1O/QZ/QR/QW/IN

Publisher's Acknowledgments

Project Editor: Traci Cumbay
Composition Services: Indianapolis Composition Services Department
Cover Photo: © Michael Pole/CORBIS

Table of Contents

Introduction

● ●

*C*onsider these facts:

- ✔ One American dies of heart disease every 33 seconds — amounting to almost one million deaths every year.
- ✔ Almost one in four Americans has one or more types of heart disease.
- ✔ Considering all risk factors for heart disease — high blood pressure, high cholesterol, smoking, being overweight, physical inactivity — not one family in America is left untouched by heart disease.
- ✔ Regardless of your age, sex, ethnicity, and current heart health, you can acquire the knowledge and take action to work toward a healthier heart and the benefits that go with it.

As you hold this book in your hand to read these facts, your heart is beating away in your chest, sustaining your life. Although it's about the size of a clenched adult fist and weighs less than a pound, your heart beats 40 million times a year and generates enough force to lift you 100 miles into the atmosphere. What an amazing — and absolutely essential — machine!

About This Book

Heart Disease For Dummies, Pocket Edition, is a common-sense guide for everyone. In this book, I give you some advice, simple diagrams, and yes, even an occasional stern lecture about simple things that you can do every day to maximize your cardiac function. You also find some basic strategies and lifestyle practices to reduce your risk of the major forms of heart disease.

If you (or your loved ones) already have heart disease or if you want to lower your risk of getting it, you have come to the right place. I run the largest exercise, nutrition, and cardiac lifestyle research laboratory in the world. I am also a board-certified cardiologist and editor of the major intensive-care textbook in the United States. I personally have performed thousands of heart catheterizations and taken care of many people with all forms of heart disease.

I rely on that background and the many important conversations that I've had with patients to give you some simple advice about the common conditions related to heart disease. I explore some facts related to coronary artery disease, angina, heart attacks, hypertension, heart failure, and many other cardiac conditions. Along the way, I hope to answer those questions that I am commonly asked and those I suspect many of my patients had but may have been afraid to ask.

When you were born, you were given one heart and one life. Making the best of both is up to you. This book's goal is to provide simple, straightforward information and answers to help you do just that.

Foolish Assumptions

The book assumes that you know nothing about heart disease. You won't suddenly have to face a term that isn't explained and that you never heard of before. You can pick and choose how much you want to know about a subject, but the key points are clearly marked.

Icons Used in This Book

This icon signals physiological and scientific information about the heart. But don't worry — all technical stuff is presented in plain English.

You find facts, practices, and insights that promote or enhance heart health alongside this icon.

This icon indicates practical suggestions you can put to work to help you reach your heart-health goals.

Think of this icon as a caution flag.

Where to Go from Here

Where you go from here depends on your needs. You're welcome to read straight through or to skip around the book, reading whatever interests you or addresses your questions.

If you want even more information on heart disease, from treatments to picking out the right doctor for you to managing heart disease through lifestyle changes, check out the full-size version of *Heart Disease For Dummies,* 2nd Edition (Wiley). Simply head to your local bookseller or go to www.dummies.com.

Chapter 1

Confronting the No. 1 Health Threat

. . . .

In This Chapter

▶ Reviewing the good and bad news about heart disease

▶ Finding out that you can improve your heart health

▶ Assessing your risk of a first heart attack

. . . .

*W*hy is the heart so magical for us? Why do we tell our loved ones that they live inside our hearts? Why do we say that someone with enormous courage has "tremendous heart"? Why are lovers said to die of a broken heart? Everyone has an emotional attachment to this miraculous pump that is inconceivable for any other organ. Would you ever think about your lungs or kidneys or pancreas in this way? Of course not. Humans seem to have a built-in sense of the heart's importance. And cardiovascular disease in all its forms is the biggest threat to our hearts.

Exploring How Heart Disease Affects Your Life

The heart captivates our imagination for good reason — human health, daily performance, and life itself depend on the heart. The heart and the cardiovascular system have amazing sophistication, strength, and durability. At the same time, the health of the heart rests in a fragile balance. When even small parts of its complex machinery are a little bit out of whack, the heart can cause great discomfort, pain, and even death.

Facing the bad news about heart disease

Heart disease is public health enemy number one in America. In one or another of its manifestations, heart disease touches virtually every family in the United States. Consider these startling facts:

- Almost 60 million Americans — almost one in every four — have one or more types of heart disease.

- Heart disease and stroke cause more than one of every two deaths — more deaths than all other diseases combined.

- An individual is more than 10 times more likely to die of heart disease than in an accident and more than 30 times as likely to die of heart disease than of AIDS.

- Heart disease is an equal-opportunity killer. It is the leading cause of death in men and women and all ethnic and racial groups in the United States.

- If money is the most important thing in your life, you might like to know that the yearly estimated cost of cardiovascular disease in the United States is $286.5 billion.

As a cardiologist, I've seen these statistics made all too real in the lives of too many patients. But I've also seen what people can do to take charge of heart health at all stages, from working to lower their risk of developing heart disease to learning how to control and live well with advanced coronary artery disease (CAD) and its varied manifestations.

Seizing the good news about controlling heart disease

The bad-news facts about heart disease are real, but they aren't the only news. Extensive research proves that you can do many things in your daily life and in working with your physician to use the latest medical science that can preserve and maximize the health of your heart — even if you already have heart disease. Consider these good-news facts:

- ✔ People who are physically active on a regular basis cut their risk of heart disease in half.

- ✔ People who stop smoking cigarettes can return their risk of heart disease and stroke to almost normal levels within five years after stopping.

- ✔ Overweight people who lose as little as 5 percent to 10 percent of their body weight can substantially lower their risk of heart disease.

- ✔ Simple changes in what you eat can lower blood cholesterol.

- ✔ The number of deaths from heart disease declined 20 percent during the last decade — a decline largely based on lifestyle changes.

Working with your physician to control heart disease

Even if you have CAD or have had a heart attack, clinical research shows that working with your physician in a supervised program to reduce your risk factors for heart disease is highly beneficial and even life saving. Take a look at what research reveals about how you can improve your health:

- ✔ If you have CAD, modifying risk factors such as high blood pressure, high blood cholesterol, physical inactivity, and being overweight can reduce your risk of a future heart attack or the need for coronary artery bypass surgery and add years to your life.

- ✔ In clinical studies, people who experienced a heart attack or unstable angina and who lowered their total cholesterol by 18 percent and LDL cholesterol by 25 percent experienced a 24 percent decrease in death from cardiovascular disease when compared to a control group. The need for bypass surgery was reduced by 20 percent.

- ✔ Appropriate physical activity or exercise improves the ability to perform activities comfortably for people with angina and people who've had heart attacks or even coronary surgery.

- ✔ Weight loss can help lower cholesterol levels and control blood pressure and diabetes — conditions that contribute to the continued progress of heart disease.

- ✔ If you smoke and have had a heart attack, quitting smoking significantly reduces your risk of having a second heart attack or experiencing sudden death.

Identifying Six Risk Factors That You Can Control

Although risk factors often are classified as *major* factors or *other* factors, dividing them into the ones you *can* modify and the ones you *cannot* modify probably is more enlightening. So that's the way I discuss them, starting with the risk factors that you can tackle successfully.

High blood pressure

Landmark studies conducted in the 1960s put to rest any serious doubt that elevated blood pressure, or *hypertension,* represents a substantial risk for developing CAD and stroke. Hypertension appears to be particularly dangerous in terms of the likelihood of developing a stroke. (For more about stroke, see Chapter 3.)

Once again, the good news is that daily habits and practices, such as appropriate weight control, sound nutrition, and regular physical activity can profoundly diminish the likelihood of your ever developing hypertension in the first place and can significantly contribute to the effective treatment of elevated blood pressure. (For more about these healthful practices, see Chapter 7.) In fact, controlling blood pressure within normal levels is an important part of both primary and secondary prevention of heart disease (and kidney disease, the other great health risk of hypertension).

Elevated cholesterol

By now, almost everyone knows having a high cholesterol level in your blood is a bad thing. When it comes to being at risk of developing CAD, however, an elevated level of blood cholesterol is one of a number of *lipid problems* (problems with fats in the blood) that significantly elevate your risk of heart disease. The abnormalities that are particularly dangerous include elevated total cholesterol, elevated LDL cholesterol, low HDL cholesterol, elevated triglycerides, or any combination of the four.

The good news is that by following appropriate lifestyle measures and, in some instances, using effective medicines that now are available, this risk factor for CAD can be effectively managed.

Smoking

With all the information available about health, heart disease, and cigarette smoking, smokers who fail to understand that smoking poses a very serious threat to their health must have been hiding incommunicado in a wilderness cave for the last 40 years. Reams of data present a very stark, negative picture: Cigarette smoking (and the use of other tobacco products) is the leading cause of premature death in the United States each year, claiming more than 400,000 lives.

The health consequences of cigarette smoking are severe. Smoking

✔ Triples the risk of developing heart disease and increases the risk of developing lung cancer by a whopping 3,000 percent.

✔ Increases the risk of harming the health of others. Individuals with CAD can have angina attacks provoked merely by being in a smoke-filled room.

✔ Tends to lower HDL cholesterol (the good guys).

In an otherwise bleak picture, the outstanding good news is that stopping smoking

✔ Lowers the risk of developing CAD and significantly improves the health outlook for individuals who have heart disease.

✔ Can add two to three years to your life expectancy.

> ✔ Improves blood lipids. In one study, LDL cholesterol decreased more than 5 percent and HDL cholesterol increased more than 3 percent in individuals who stopped cigarette smoking.

Inactivity

In 1994, faced with overwhelming evidence, the American Heart Association added the first new major factor in 25 years — a physically inactive lifestyle — to the list of risks for developing CAD.

Physical inactivity is defined as a major factor, in part, because it also contributes significantly to a number of the other major risk factors, such as high blood pressure, perhaps elevated blood cholesterol, and often obesity. But if you get off your duff and get active, you can turn this sad picture around. (See Chapter 7 for help.) A physically active lifestyle not only reduces the specific risk that inactivity poses for heart disease, it also helps lessen or eradicate several of the other major risk factors for heart disease.

Obesity

In 1998, obesity joined the list of major independent risk factors for developing CAD. Like physical inactivity, obesity also contributes to many other risk factors, including hypertension and elevated cholesterol, and other abnormal lipid levels.

More than one in every three adults is now considered obese. By *obese,* I mean weighing at least 20 percent more than desirable body weight. That's not as fat as most people think, either. For example, if your optimal weight is 150 pounds and you weigh 180 — just 30 pounds overweight — you are technically obese even if you think you still look pretty good.

Being obese increases the risk of CAD in a number of different ways that include:

- ✔ Interacting negatively with many other risk factors for developing CAD, such as high blood pressure, Type 2 diabetes, and cholesterol problems.

- ✔ Clustering of risk factors. Obese people are particularly susceptible to a clustering of risk factors.

- ✔ Serving as a forerunner to dangerous lipid abnormalities that increase the risk of heart disease, including elevated blood triglycerides, elevated LDL cholesterol levels, and depressed HDL cholesterol levels.

Carrying extra weight around the abdomen (sometimes called *abdominal obesity* or *apple-shaped obesity*) is particularly dangerous in terms of its risk of coronary heart disease.

If you're overweight, regardless of whether you have heart disease, you need to make a point of talking to your doctor about whether you show signs of having other risk factors for heart disease in addition to obesity. The odds are that you do.

If you've been diagnosed with heart disease and are overweight, then be sure to discuss these issues with your physician. Weight loss in and of itself is a highly effective way of reducing multiple risk factors for heart disease.

Remember, obese people do not die because they are too fat; they die of heart disease.

Diabetes mellitus

Approximately 17 million people in the United States, or 6.2 percent of the population, suffer from diabetes mellitus. About 90 percent to 95 percent of these individuals have Type 2 or adult onset diabetes. Diabetes represents a significant risk factor for coronary heart disease. In fact, coronary heart disease is by far the leading cause of death in individuals with diabetes.

Individuals with diabetes often have multiple blood lipid abnormalities, including elevated blood triglycerides and elevated LDL cholesterol and a depressed HDL cholesterol. Having this particular constellation of lipid abnormalities spells triple trouble! For reasons that to date are not totally clear, women with diabetes have an even greater risk of developing heart disease than men with diabetes.

Recent compelling research shows that individuals who have some degree of insulin resistance or glucose intolerance — test results that put them in the "prediabetic" category — also have elevated risk of heart disease.

By working with your physician if you have diabetes, however, you can lower many of the complications of diabetes and also control your blood lipids. Daily steps that you can take to help you control diabetes include weight loss if you're overweight, regular physical activity, and proper nutritional habits.

Watching for Risk Factors That You Cannot Modify

Now I come to three risk factors that you can't modify: your age, gender, and family history (see the list that follows). Having one or more of these nonmodifiable risk factors makes it particularly important that you pay close attention to the risk factors that you *can* modify.

✔ **Age:** Age is considered a significant risk factor for CAD for men who are older than 45 and for women who are older than 55 or have undergone premature menopause.

✔ **Gender:** Men are more likely to develop CAD than women. Furthermore, the onset of symptoms of CAD typically occurs ten years later in women than in men; however, pointing out that CAD remains the number-one killer in *both* men and women in the United States is important. CAD becomes particularly prevalent in women after menopause. After age 65, men and women have approximately the same risk for developing CAD.

✔ **Family history:** CAD tends to occur more frequently in some families than in others. Coming from a family in which premature coronary heart disease has occurred clearly increases your risk of developing CAD. By *premature coronary heart disease* I mean a diagnosed heart attack or a sudden death before age 55 in males or age 65 in females. Having a first-degree relative (father, mother, brother, or sister) who fits this description qualifies as a risk factor.

Multiplying Risks — Double Trouble and More

One aspect of risk factors that makes them particularly dangerous is that their effects multiply, rather than merely add up, whenever you exhibit two or more of them.

Individuals with only a single risk factor actually double their chances of developing heart disease. When two risk factors are present, the possibility quadruples. And, worse yet, when three risk factors join forces, the possibility of your developing heart disease increases 8 to 20 times! If you think that's bad news, listen to this: Having two and three risk factors is not unusual. In fact, risk factors have a distinct tendency to occur in clusters.

For most risk factors, what you helped create, you can also change through:

- ✔ **Primary prevention:** By controlling risk factors before the onslaught of CAD, you can substantially lower your chances of ever developing coronary heart disease by lowering your blood pressure, lowering your cholesterol, quitting smoking, exercising, and losing weight.

- ✔ **Secondary prevention:** If you already have CAD, attempting to bring these same factors under control usually decreases your risk of having further complications and manifestations from CAD.

Controlling or treating a particular risk factor may mean different things for different people. One size does not fit all. For example, a young woman with a mildly elevated cholesterol level — say 215 mg/dl — but no other risk factors may require only some healthful modifications in diet and physical activity. On the other hand, a 60-year-old man who's already suffered a heart attack and has the same level of elevated cholesterol may require immediate, aggressive treatment to lower his cholesterol levels.

Assessing Your Risk of a First Heart Attack

Based on data from the Framingham Heart Study, the longest and largest population study of heart disease, the test that follows helps you assess your risk of having a first heart attack, gives you a good idea of how you can modify your risk factors, and may highlight topics for you to talk about with your physician at your next checkup. You do have a regular checkup scheduled, don't you?

Benefiting from heart health

Taking control of your heart health offers other wonderful upsides for living well that include

✔ **Improving your overall health:** Many of the steps that benefit your heart health also improve your total health and fitness, to say nothing of your good looks.

✔ **Increasing functionality:** Use it or lose it, goes the old saying. The healthier your heart, the greater the probability that you can stay active, mobile, and engaged in pursuits that interest you for a long, long time.

✔ **Increasing economic benefits:** The healthier you are, the lower your health-care costs, and the more money in your pocket for fun things.

✔ **Increasing longevity:** Keeping your heart healthy is not an iron-clad guarantee that you'll live longer, but considering the mortality rates of people with heart disease, even card-carrying "Dummies" can figure out that keeping your heart as healthy as possible can keep the grim reaper away longer.

✔ **Having more fun:** Nothing slows you down or scares the family like a heart attack. Angina pain, angioplasty, coronary artery bypass surgery, and other common outcomes of heart disease aren't picnics in the park, either. Working for heart health and controlling heart disease can help you avoid these problems.

First Heart Attack Risk Test

This test can help you figure out your risk of having a first heart attack. Fill in your points for each risk factor. Then total them to find out your level of risk.

_____**Age (in years) Men:** Younger than 35, 0 points; 35 to 39, 1 point; 40 to 48, 2 points; 49 to 53, 3 points; and 54 and older, 4 points.

_____**Age (in years) Women:** Younger than 42, 0 points; 42 to 44, 1 point; 45 to 54, 2 points; 55 to 73, 3 points; 74 and older, 4 points.

_____**Family History:** A family history of heart disease or heart attacks before age 60 — 2 points.

_____**Inactive Lifestyle:** I rarely exercise or do anything physically demanding — 1 point.

_____**Weight:** I weigh 20 (or more) pounds more than my ideal weight — 1point.

_____**Smoking:** I'm a smoker — 1 point.

_____**Diabetic:** Male diabetic, 1 point; female diabetic, 2 points.

_____**Total Cholesterol Level:** Less than 240 mg/dl, 0 points; 240 to 315 mg/dl, 1 point; more than 315 mg/dl, 2 points.

_____**HDL Level (good cholesterol):** Less than 30 mg/dl, 2 points; 30 to 39 mg/dl, 1 point; 40 to 60mg/dl, 0 points; more than 60 mg/dl, 1 point.

_____**Blood Pressure:** I don't take blood pressure medication; my blood pressure is *(use your top or higher blood pressure number):* less than 140 mmHg, 0 points; 140 to 170 mmHg, 1 point; greater than 170 mmHg, 2 points; or, I'm currently taking blood pressure medication — 1 point.

_____**Total Points**

If you scored 4 points or more, you may be above the average risk of a first heart attack compared to the general adult population. The more points you score, the higher your risk. (Based on data from the Framingham Study, as adapted by Bristol-Myers Squibb.)

If you scored 4 points or more and haven't had a recent checkup, scheduling one soon is a good idea. You may also want to take your risk assessment results in to discuss with your physician.

Chapter 2

Touring the Heart and Cardiovascular System

. . . .

In This Chapter

▶ Understanding how the heart works

▶ Defining the components of the cardiovascular system

▶ Checking out the role of the nervous system

▶ Linking some typical heart problems to the heart's anatomy

▶ Spiraling down the slope from health to heart disease

. . . .

*T*he average adult heart is about the size of a clenched fist and weighs less than a pound. But your life depends on your heart. The heart is the engine that keeps your body functioning. When disease or injury strikes the heart, the body's ability to function declines as the heart's ability declines.

In this chapter, I discuss how your heart and cardio-vascular system are structured — their anatomy and how they accomplish their amazing work.

Pumping for Life: The Heart

The heart is located in the center of the chest cavity. About one-third rests beneath the breastbone, or *sternum,* and two-thirds rests to the left of the midline of the body. The breastbone, rib cage, muscles, and other structures of the chest wall protect the heart.

In the average adult, the heart pumps 5 quarts of blood per minute at rest and 25 to 30 quarts per minute at maximum effort. In highly trained athletes working at maximum effort, the amount of blood pumped per minute can run as high as 40 quarts.

The heart muscle

The walls of the heart are made up of a unique muscle called the myocardium (*myo* = muscle and *cardium* = heart; pronounced my-o-*car*-dee-um). This muscle is the only one of its kind in the body because it must be supplied with oxygenated blood at all times to survive.

Other muscles, such as those of the arms and legs, although still highly dependent on oxygenated blood, can perform briefly in the absence of oxygen (as when you dash from your car to the store during a rainshower). The heart is denied this luxury. For the heart to keep beating, arteries that feed the heart, the *coronary arteries,* must deliver a continuous supply of oxygenated blood. That's why the narrowing of these arteries, which is known as *coronary artery disease* (CAD), is so dangerous to the heart.

When the coronary arteries grow narrower, a series of adverse events ensues, starting with *angina* (*an*-juh-uh), or chest pain, and ranging all the way to heart attack and, potentially, sudden death.

The heart as a pump

The heart is a magnificent four-chambered pump that has two jobs:

✔ Pumping blood to the lungs to get oxygen

✔ Pumping the oxygenated blood to the rest of the body

To fulfill these tasks, the heart has a left and a right side (as shown in Figure 2-1), each with one main pumping chamber called a *ventricle* located in the lower part of it.

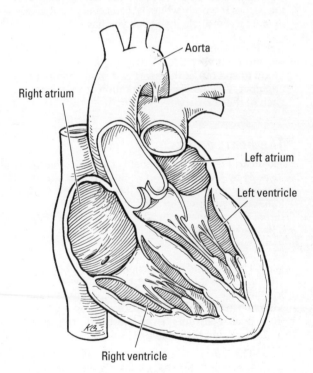

Aorta

Right atrium

Left atrium

Left ventricle

Right ventricle

Figure 2-1: The four chambers of the heart.

Sitting above the left and right ventricles are two small booster pumps called *atria* (or *atrium,* when you're talking about just one). The right ventricle pumps deoxygenated blood, which returns from the body through veins and the right atrium, out into the lungs where it receives a new supply of oxygen. The blood then returns to the heart, first entering the left atrium and then the left ventricle. The left ventricle pumps oxygenated blood through the arterial system out to the rest of the body where it feeds every vital organ — in fact, every single living cell you have.

A thick muscular wall called the *septum* separates the left and right ventricles. Valves regulate the flow of blood in and out of the heart and from chamber to chamber. Various disease conditions can damage each of these structures.

The heart valves

The heart has four valves that act a bit like cardiac traffic cops by directing the way blood flows, how much of it flows, and when to stop it from flowing. Take a look at the positions of the four valves and how they direct blood flow through the heart in Figure 2-2.

The four valves are

- ✔ The *tricuspid* (try-*cuhs*-pid) valve, so called because it has three cusps, or flaps, opens to enable blood to flow into the right ventricle when the heart is relaxed and closes when the heart contracts to prevent blood from going back into the body.

- ✔ The *mitral* valve (*my*-trul), which resembles a bishop's miter (hat), controls the blood flow between the left atrium and the left ventricle. (The next time you see the Pope in full regalia, think of his hat as resembling the structure of a mitral valve in the heart.)

✔ The *pulmonic* (pull-*mon*-ik) valve controls the flow of blood from the right ventrical to the pulmonary artery supplying the lungs. (This valve is called *pulmonic* because the Latin word for lungs is the root word for *pulmonary.*)

✔ The *aortic* (ay-*or*-tik) valve, which separates the left ventricle from the aorta, opens to enable blood flow to the body when the heart contracts and closes when the heart relaxes to prevent blood from flowing back into the heart.

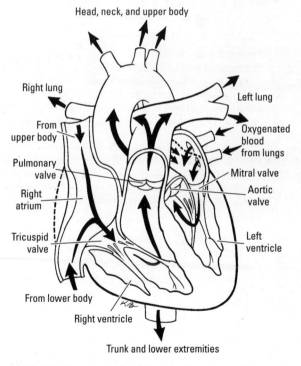

Figure 2-2: The valves of the heart and how they work.

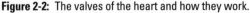

Disease and injury can cause heart valves to leak, narrow, or otherwise malfunction, disrupting the heart's ability to pump blood efficiently. (I discuss valve problems in Chapter 4.)

The coronary arteries

Three large coronary arteries and their many branches supply blood to the heart. As you can see in Figure 2-3, two coronary arteries branch off one main trunk, which is called the *left main coronary artery.* One of these branches runs down the front of the heart, so in med-speak, it is naturally called the *left anterior descending artery.* (*Anterior* is just a fancy word for front.)

The second branch of the left main coronary artery circles around and supplies the side wall of the heart, so it is called the *left circumflex artery.* The third main coronary artery, which typically comes off of a separate trunk vessel, is called the *right coronary artery.* It supplies the back and bottom walls of the heart.

Significant narrowing of any of these coronary arteries causes angina, a symptom typically characterized as chest pain. (I discuss angina in detail in Chapter 3.) An acute, or sudden, blockage of one of these arteries causes a heart attack, and, as a result, the heart muscle that formerly was supplied by the blocked artery dies.

Mechanics tell you that the most important thing you can do to keep your car healthy is to change the oil frequently. Well, keeping your coronary arteries clear, free-flowing, and doing their job for the heart is the most important thing you can do to keep your heart healthy for a lifetime.

Restoring blood flow to the heart and maintaining open arteries is the objective of a number of lifestyle, medical, and surgical treatments for coronary artery disease. This book shares a number of strategies you can use that your physician may prescribe to help you achieve this goal.

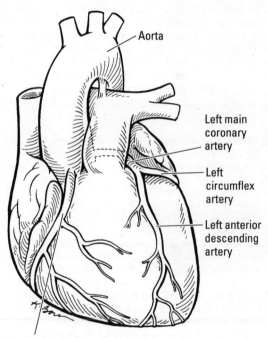

Aorta

Left main coronary artery

Left circumflex artery

Left anterior descending artery

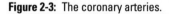

Right coronary artery

Figure 2-3: The coronary arteries.

The electrical system

Would it surprise you to hear that the beating of your heart is controlled by an electrical system? Many folks are shocked (pun and double-entendre intended) to hear that's true.

What's even more exciting is that your cardiac electric company is the mechanism that enables pacemakers and defibrillators to work. This electrical system is controlled by a group of specialized cells that spontaneously discharge, sending electrical currents down specialized nerves and tissues, thus alerting all the other heart cells that it's time to discharge and causing the heart to contract, which for most folks is at a rate of about 70 to 80 times a minute when at rest.

When any of these electrical structures becomes diseased or disordered, *arrhythmias* (ay-*rith*-mee-uhz), or heart rhythm disturbances, occur. (See Chapter 3 for more about arrhythmias.)

The pericardium

The entire heart is positioned in a thin sac called the *pericardium* (*peri* = around and *cardium* = heart; pronounced per-ry-*car*-dee-um). The thin-walled pericardium normally rests right up against the walls of the heart and is lubricated by a thin layer of body fluids that enable the heart to slide easily within it. However, this sac around the heart can become inflamed, resulting in chest discomfort or even compromised heart function. (You can check out these conditions, known as *pericarditis,* in Chapter 4.)

The Cardiovascular System

A pump is useless without the rest of the plumbing, which in your body is called the *cardiovascular system*. In the sections that follow, you can take a quick look at how it all fits together and functions.

The lungs

The lungs rest on either side of the heart and take up most of the space in the chest cavity, as shown in Figure 2-4. The lungs are composed of an intricate series of air sacs surrounded by a complex, highly branching network of blood vessels.

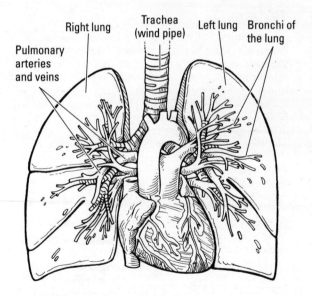

Figure 2-4: The heart and lungs.

Their sole purpose in life is to receive the deoxygenated blood from the heart, chock the red corpuscles
full of fresh oxygen, and send them back to the heart
for delivery to the body. This heart-to-lung-to-heart
circuit functions as a low-pressure system to facilitate
the rapid flow and reoxygenation of enormous amounts
of blood. What that means is that the heart doesn't
have to exert very great force with each contraction
to move blood through this system.

A clot in a blood vessel in the lungs, otherwise known
as a *pulmonary embolism,* and high blood pressure in
the lungs' arteries, *pulmonary hypertension,* are two
cardiac conditions related to the lungs. (For more
about these conditions, see Chapter 4.)

The arteries

As oxygenated blood returns to the left side of the
heart, it's pumped out to the body through the *aorta,*
the main artery of the body, and into the rest of the
arterial system to feed the entire body with oxygenated
blood. Because the body is fairly large compared to
the size of the heart, the heart exerts enough force to
push oxygenated blood throughout the body. However,
arteries also have muscular walls that help push the
blood along. The force exerted against resistance of
the artery walls creates a high-pressure system that is
very *elastic* to allow the arteries to expand or contract
to meet the needs of various organs and muscles
regardless of whether they're working or at rest.

So each time the left ventricle contracts, pumping
blood into the arterial system, the arteries, in turn,
expand to accept the surge of blood. However, this
expansion of the arterial system doesn't occur as
rapidly as the heart contracts. Therefore, when the
heart relaxes, pressure still is in the arterial system and
blood continues to move forward or out to the body.

The contraction of the left ventricle is called *systole* (*sis*-tuh-lee). When the heart relaxes, the pressure falls somewhat as the blood continues to flow in the arterial system. This relaxation of the heart is called *diastole* (dye-*ass*-tuh-lee). Your *blood pressure* is measured by the amount of pressure in the arteries during the systole (contraction) and the diastole (relaxation).

The capillaries

The arterial system divides and redivides into a system of ever smaller branches to distribute nourishing blood to each individual cell, ultimately ending up in a network of microscopic vessels called *capillaries,* which deliver oxygenated blood to the working cells of every organ and muscle in the body. This amazing network of branching microscopic vessels puts even the most complex digital network to shame! For example, a section of body tissue no bigger than the head of a pin has between 2,000 and 3,000 capillaries.

The veins

After oxygen leaves the capillary system, the deoxygenated blood and waste products from the cells are carried back through the body in the *veins.* The veins from the legs ultimately come together in a very large vein in the middle of the body called the *inferior vena cava* (*vee*-nuh *cay*-vuh), and all the veins in the upper part of the body come together in a large vein called the *superior vena cava.* These veins discharge blood into the right atrium of the heart to be pumped into the right ventricle and out to the lungs again to start the whole process over again. This circular flow of blood through the heart is illustrated earlier in Figure 2-2.

How the Nervous System Controls Heart Rate

In addition to its internal electrical system, the heart has profound linkages to the nervous system that provide additional control of the heart rate. Two main branches of the involuntary nervous system interact with the heart — the sympathetic nervous system and the parasympathetic nervous system. In simple terms, the *sympathetic nervous system* helps the heart speed up, and the *parasympathetic nervous system* helps the heart slow down. I discuss rhythm problems in Chapter 3.

Sympathetic nervous system

The sympathetic nervous system typically directs the heart to speed up during periods of exercise or strong emotion. It acts through direct nerve links to the heart and through chemical substances that reach the heart through the blood stream. In everyday speech, you can feel your adrenaline pumping.

When the heart speeds up, that quickened pace is known in medicine as *tacchycardia* (*tack*-ih-*car*-dee-uh). Of course, this is highly beneficial when you're exercising, but it's not so good when the accelerated rate results from disordered electrical impulses found in many people with heart disease. (See Chapter 3 for further discussion of heart rhythm problems.)

Parasympathetic nervous system

The parasympathetic branch of the nervous system acts as a trusty, unobtrusive housekeeper by keeping such functions as breathing and digestion perking along without any need for conscious thought on your part. Imagine how complex life would be if you had to stop and think each time you wanted to breathe. The parasympathetic nervous system can also direct the heart to slow down through direct nerve links to the heart and through release of a chemical called acetylcholine into the bloodstream.

The slowing of the heart is called *bradycardia* (bray-dee-*car*-dee-uh). When individuals are in great shape physically, they may have a healthy bradycardia. However, in certain diseased states, the heart rate can be too slow, resulting in inadequate blood flow to the tissues.

In certain circumstances, the parasympathetic nervous system can even be tricked into causing an inappropriately slow heart rate. The resulting brief period of inadequate blood flow to the brain usually causes a fainting episode. Fainting is the brain's safety valve because when it decides the heart is not sending it enough blood, the brain sends the body crashing to the ground, where in a horizontal position, the brain automatically gets its share of the blood flow regardless of whether the heart is going fast or slow.

Inviting Heart Disease: The Couch Potato Connection

Now that you know what all the parts of the cardiovascular system are, I can show you how they work together and how easy starting down the slippery slope that leads toward heart disease can be. You can start with the favorite position of most Americans — relaxing on the couch.

The view from the couch

While you're sitting still, your heart is beating at 70 to 80 contractions per minute (unless you're very fit, but more about that later). With each contraction, the right ventricle discharges about three-quarters of the blood it contains into the vessels of the lungs, where it receives oxygen. At the same time, the left ventricle is discharging about three-quarters of the blood that it contains into the aorta and arterial system to feed the oxygen to all the organs and muscles. All four heart valves work together to control blood flow into and out of the heart, making sure that no blood flows in the wrong direction.

The arterial system dilates, or expands, each time the left ventricle empties into it and speeds blood on its way to the various working tissues. How much blood goes to each tissue is determined by what that particular muscle or organ needs to do. When you eat a big meal, for example, the heart, brain, parasympathetic nervous system, and arteries all decide that more blood needs to go to the organs in the gastrointestinal tract to help them with the work of digesting that low-fat, cardiac-healthy meal you just ate.

The view from the track

Say that after reading this book and consulting with your physician, you decide that you're going to exercise regularly. (Good idea!) Exercise poses a different challenge to the heart compared to rest. Extra blood flow must go to muscles used in exercising and to the coronary arteries that feed the heart muscle itself so that it can pump out the extra blood required during your exercise exertion.

Fortunately, this extra work is no problem for a healthy heart. Once again, all systems work in concert. Extra blood is pumped from the heart, and extra blood flows down the coronary arteries, which dilate to accept this extra flow. The heart valves continue to direct the blood in the proper direction, and the electrical system, with a little boost from the nervous system, starts generating more beats per minute. At the same time, the cardiac muscle relaxes a little bit, enabling more blood to be pumped out during each beat.

In addition, the nervous system, in conjunction with the arterial system, causes

- ✔ Some parts of the arterial circulation to expand or dilate, sending more blood to the working muscles that need it.
- ✔ Other parts to constrict or narrow, diverting blood away from areas where it is not as active during exertion.

If you exert yourself on a regular basis, your heart and the rest of your cardiovascular system begin to become more efficient and prepare for the regular exercise sessions. That's true even if you've been diagnosed with heart disease or had a heart attack or other heart event. For that reason, physicians prescribe specific types of carefully monitored activities and exercises as part of treatment and rehabilitation programs for heart disease.

Sliding down the Slippery Slope toward Heart Disease

When all parts of the heart and cardiovascular system are healthy and functioning well together, it is a beautiful system. But the heart is a muscle. And like any muscle, it works best when you keep it in shape and avoid injury.

The conditioned heart

A conditioned heart is stronger and better able to meet the demands the body places on it. Human bodies were designed to be in motion. And the motion of physical activity keeps the heart well tuned, the benefits of which are numerous:

- ✔ Literally hundreds of studies have shown that individuals who adopt the simple habit of daily physical activity substantially reduce their risk of developing various heart problems, most notably coronary artery disease.

- ✔ The conditioned heart enables individuals to accomplish the activities of daily living with comfort and without running out of breath and energy.

- ✔ The more conditioned the heart, the lower the resting heart rate, and the less work the heart has to do in a lifetime.

- ✔ Studies also show that, with appropriate activity, hearts damaged by disease or injury can regain conditioning that enhances health and function and may even contribute to the reversal of some aspects of disease.

The deconditioned heart

In contrast to the active individual, the individual who leads a sedentary lifestyle can actually experience a deconditioned heart. The deconditioned heart is less efficient at doing its work and has to work harder to get adequate blood flow throughout the body.

For many people a deconditioned heart is the first step in a slow slide down the long slope toward a sick heart. You're a prime candidate for a deconditioned heart if you answer "yes" to these questions or others like them:

✔ Do you avoid the stairs because climbing two or three flights leaves you extremely short of breath?

✔ Do you circle a parking lot numerous times looking for a space right in front of the store to make sure that you don't have to walk much?

✔ Do you watch sports on television rather than participate in them with friends and family?

✔ On a nice day, do you pop a DVD into the player rather than take a walk?

The diseased heart

A sedentary lifestyle coupled with unhealthy practices such as poor nutrition, weight gain, cigarette smoking, or certain other health conditions, such as high blood pressure, high cholesterol, or diabetes, can severely alter the basic cardiac structures and lead to a disordered anatomy that can create a very unhappy destiny. A short list of the things that can go wrong includes blocked arteries, high cholesterol, high blood pressure, angina, heart attack, heart failure, and sudden death. The bottom line: Many of the cardiac problems that people experience are brought on by years of neglect and failure to abide by even the most basic of cardiac-healthy lifestyle principles. (Nature makes a few mistakes, too, but even in those cases, personal choices often complicate the problem.)

The good news is that even if you've been diagnosed as at risk for heart disease or as having it, and even if you've experienced specific heart problems, paying attention to the basic principles of a cardiac-healthy lifestyle in conjunction with the medications and procedures of your treatment plan can help you turn things around.

Chapter 3

Identifying the Many Forms of Heart Disease

. . . .

In This Chapter

▶ Understanding what causes coronary artery disease

▶ Determining the causes and effects of angina and unstable angina

▶ Finding out about heart attack

▶ Looking into arrhythmia

▶ Defining heart failure

▶ Investigating stroke

. . . .

*I*n this chapter, you get some basic information to help you understand coronary heart disease and its manifestations, including angina and heart attack, arrhythmia, stroke, and others. You may find these discussions a little scary, and I almost hope that you do because I'd like nothing more than for you to take your heart health seriously. I want this chapter to inspire you to learn more about how to put yourself in the best possible shape for steering clear of these serious conditions.

Defining CAD, or Atherosclerosis

Coronary artery disease (also known as CAD, *coronary heart disease — CHD, coronary atherosclerosis,* or *coronary arteriosclerosis*) is the slow, progressive narrowing of the three main arteries (and their branches) that supply blood to the heart. This narrowing of the arteries gradually starves the heart muscle of the high level of oxygenated blood that it needs to function properly. A lack of adequate blood supply to the heart typically produces symptoms that range from angina and unstable angina (see "Investigating Angina" and "Looking into Unstable Angina," later in this chapter) to heart attack or sudden death.

Narrowing arteries that are characteristic of CAD result from the gradual buildup of fatty deposits called *plaque,* or *lesions,* on their interior walls. *Atherosclerosis,* the most common medical term for CAD, comes from two Greek words — *athero* (paste, gruel) and *sclerosis* (hardness) — that may give you a graphic image of hardened sludge. Not a pretty picture, is it? But it's an apt image for these deposits of cholesterol, other fats, cellular wastes, platelets, calcium, and other substances.

These deposits typically start with fatty streaks and grow to large bumps that distort the artery and block its interior where the blood must flow. Some plaques are stable and others are unstable or vulnerable to cracking or rupturing, which often leads to an artery-blocking blood clot and subsequent heart attack. I discuss the whole process in the next section.

The disease process that leads to advanced atherosclerosis starts with small changes in the artery wall and takes years to develop to a point where the narrowing arteries may produce symptoms or negatively affect your health.

Investigating Angina

When coronary artery disease progresses enough to significantly diminish the blood flow to heart tissue, it produces *angina pectoris,* which is commonly called angina. *Angina* typically is a discomfort felt in the chest, often beneath the breastbone (or sternum) or in nearby areas such as the neck, jaw, back, or arms.

- ✔ Individuals often describe the chest discomfort as a "squeezing sensation," "vicelike," "constricting," or "a heavy pressure on the chest." (In fact, the term *angina* comes from a Greek word that means "strangling" — a strangling pain.)

- ✔ Angina often is brought on by physical exertion or strong emotions and typically is relieved within several minutes by resting or using nitroglycerin.

- ✔ Some individuals may experience angina as a symptom different from chest discomfort or in addition to it. Shortness of breath, faintness, or fatigue may also be manifestations of angina, although if chest pain is absent, they may be called *anginal equivalents.*

- ✔ When chest pain occurs at rest, it usually is classified as *unstable angina.*

And just how do you pronounce the word? Some people say "an-*ji*-nuh" and others say "*an*-juh-nuh." Either is correct. Some cardiologists may be a little snobby about their preference (who, us?), but pay them no mind.

Although the most common form of angina results from the slow, progressive narrowing of the coronary arteries from coronary artery disease, two other rare forms of angina also may occur:

- **Variant angina,** or *Prinzmetal's angina,* which is named for Dr. Myron Prinzmetal, the cardiologist who first described this condition in 1959, occurs when the coronary arteries actually spasm, or contract suddenly. Although such episodes may occur in a normal coronary artery, spasm is most likely to occur where fatty plaque already is present. Treatment for this condition is similar to what is done for the more common form of angina, although a greater emphasis may be placed on medicines that decrease spasm (for example, calcium channel blockers, and nitrates).

- **Microvascular angina,** recently discovered, results from narrowing of tiny vessels in the heart while the major coronary arteries remain largely free of plaque. It is usually treated medically with common angina medications.

All chest pain is not angina and does not involve the heart. Various conditions involving other structures in the chest can occasionally cause chest discomfort. In many of these instances, the characteristics of the pain distinguish it from angina. Pain typically is not coming from the heart if it

- ✔ Is extremely short in duration (lasting less than ten seconds).

- ✔ Feels like it is on the surface of the chest wall rather than deep inside.

- ✔ Is sharp, stabbing pain.

- ✔ Is not associated with exertion.

Knowing when chest pain is an emergency

People with coronary artery disease (CAD) and angina typically live with this problem for many years and discover how to manage it effectively with appropriate medicines and advice from their physicians. When angina pain changes in character, however, it can signal unstable angina or even heart attack. If you experience any of the following characteristics of chest discomfort, *you need to call 911 and be taken to a hospital immediately:*

- ✔ Pain or discomfort that is not relieved by three nitroglycerin tablets in succession, each taken five minutes apart

- ✔ Pain or discomfort that is accompanied by fainting or lightheadedness, nausea, and/or cool, clammy skin

- ✔ Pain or discomfort lasting longer than 20 minutes or that is very bad or worse than you have experienced before

If any of these symptoms occur, you need to call an ambulance and be taken immediately to a hospital. Under no circumstances should you drive yourself to the hospital.

Looking Into Unstable Angina

Although it typically results from underlying CAD and often is related to angina, unstable angina represents a significant turn for the worse. It usually is a medical emergency.

As the name suggests, *unstable angina* results when angina gets out of control. In unstable angina, the lack of blood flow and oxygen to the heart becomes acute and, therefore, very dangerous because the risk of complications such as heart attack is much greater.

 Where stable angina has typical characteristics and predictable triggers, such as exertion or strong emotion, unstable angina is characterized by one or more of the following symptoms:

✔ Anginal discomfort at rest or when awakening from sleep

✔ A significant change in the pattern of the angina where it occurs with less exertion or is more severe than before

✔ A significant increase in the severity or frequency of angina

✔ New onset, or first experience, of anginal chest pain

If you experience any one of these characteristics, you must seek immediate medical attention.

Defining Heart Attack

A heart attack, known medically as a *myocardial infarction* (MI), occurs when one of the three coronary arteries that supply oxygen-rich blood to the heart muscle *(myocardium)* becomes severely or totally blocked, usually by a blood clot. When the heart muscle doesn't receive enough oxygenated blood, it begins to die. The severity of the heart attack depends on how much of the heart is injured or dies when it occurs.

When you think you're having a heart attack, go immediately to a hospital where therapy can be initiated to save your heart muscle from dying. New clot-busting medicines, as well as procedures such as angioplasty, often can dissolve a clot that causes the heart attack, open the blood vessel, and save some or all of the heart muscle at risk.

Although some of the heart muscle usually dies during a heart attack, the remaining heart muscle continues to function and often can compensate, to a very large degree, for the heart muscle that has died.

Understanding the causes of a heart attack

Heart attack almost always is caused when a blood clot forms at the site of an existing fatty plaque that has narrowed the coronary artery. Thus, individuals are at much higher risk for heart attack if they

✔ Have a history of CAD

✔ Have experienced previous bouts of angina

✔ Have suffered a previous heart attack

The blockage that triggers a heart attack usually is caused by an acute blood clot. Most *acute blood clots* occur when one of the plaques or

fatty deposits on the artery walls cracks or ruptures (see Chapter 4). Other, much more rare causes of acute blockages in arteries supplying the heart include:

✔ Inflammation of the artery

✔ Spasm, or sudden contraction of one or more coronary arteries

✔ Certain blood-clotting abnormalities

✔ Severe spasm, acute blood clot, or other problem caused by cocaine use

Recognizing the symptoms of a heart attack

Different people experience the symptoms of a heart attack in different ways. However, typical symptoms include some or all of the following:

✔ A heavy chest pain or tightness, usually experienced in the front of the chest, beneath the sternum and often radiating to the left arm, left shoulder, or jaw

✔ Shortness of breath

✔ Nausea

✔ Sweating

✔ Clamminess, cool skin, pallor

✔ A feeling of general weakness or tiredness

In an individual who has angina, symptoms may be particularly difficult to differentiate from the chest discomfort of angina. However, when a heart attack is occurring, chest discomfort usually is more severe and may occur while the individual is at rest or less active than usual.

The signs of a heart attack often are subtle, particularly with individuals who have diabetes. Diabetics may not have the classic symptoms of chest, shoulder, or arm discomfort. Chest pain experienced by many women likewise may not present the classic symptoms.

About two-thirds of the individuals who experience an acute heart attack also experience some warning symptoms in the weeks or days preceding the acute event. They often don't realize what the warning signs were until after the event — with keen hindsight. So work on your foresight. That way you'll know the warning signs of heart attack and take them seriously. (See the nearby sidebar "Experiencing heart attack warning signs? Call 911!")

Experiencing heart attack warning signs? Call 911!

Coronary artery disease (CAD) is extremely common in men and women in the United States and particularly in individuals who are in their 40s and older. Even if you've never had a single sign of trouble, you need to call 911 and go straight to the hospital for prompt evaluation whenever you experience any of these warning signs (as described by the American Heart Association):

✔ Uncomfortable pressure, fullness, squeezing, or pain in the center of the chest lasting more than a few minutes

✔ Pain spreading to the shoulders, neck, or arms

✔ Chest discomfort with lightheadedness, fainting, sweating, nausea, or shortness of breath

Do not take a meeting. Do not put it off for an hour . . . *just call 911 and go!*

Avoiding deadly excuses for delay

You've probably heard that getting treatment during the first "golden hour" after an accident gives trauma victims the best chance of survival and full recovery. The same is true of victims of biological accidents such as heart attacks. Using any of these common excuses for delay can be deadly:

- ✔ **How embarrassing if it's just heartburn.** And what if it isn't? Don't let a little embarrassment cost your life or your health.

- ✔ **I'm not sure whether my pain fits the warning signs.** The symptoms of heart attack vary from individual to individual and can be very vague. Let the physicians decide. It's their job, and they want to do it for you.

- ✔ **I'm too young to have a heart attack.** Heart attacks can and do happen at any age.

- ✔ **The pain's not that bad; I'll wait awhile and see whether it goes away.** Don't wait! Delaying significantly increases your risk of disabling damage and death.

- ✔ **Only men get heart attacks.** Whoa, ladies! Absolutely not! Women also suffer heart attacks, and their survival rate is not as good, in part, because they delay getting medical attention.

- ✔ **I'm as healthy as a horse — I can't be having a heart attack.** Denial never stopped a heart attack. For many victims, particularly younger people, heart attacks happen suddenly and without any noticeable warning signs.

The following six-point survival plan, adapted from American Medical Association recommendations, can save your life. Take these steps if you or a loved one is experiencing the symptoms of a possible heart attack:

1. **Stop what you are doing, and sit or lie down.**

2. **If symptoms persist for more than two minutes, call your local emergency number or 911 and say that you may be having a heart attack.**

   Leave the phone off the hook so that medical personnel can locate your address in the event that you become unconscious.

3. **Take nitroglycerin, if possible.**

   If you have nitroglycerin tablets, take up to three pills under your tongue, one at a time, every five minutes, if your chest pain persists.

   If you don't have nitroglycerin, take two aspirin.

4. **Do not drive yourself (or a loved one) to the hospital if you think you are having a heart attack.**

   Ambulances have equipment and personnel who are trained to deal with individuals who are having a heart attack. Driving yourself or a loved one to the hospital is an invitation for a disaster.

5. **If the person's pulse or breathing stops, any individual trained in cardiopulmonary resuscitation (CPR) needs to immediately begin to administer it.**

   If an automated external defibrillator (AED) is available, use it. Call 911 immediately, but do not delay instituting CPR or using an AED.

6. **When you arrive at the hospital emergency room, announce clearly that you (or your loved one) may be having a heart attack and that you must be seen immediately.**

   Don't be shy about it.

Characterizing Arrhythmias

Cardiac *arrhythmias,* also called cardiac *dysrhythmias,* are irregularities or abnormalities in the beating of the heart. Arrhythmias are surprisingly common. They can arise in a wide variety of settings and can range from totally insignificant to life-threatening. In fact, if everyone were hooked up to a 24-hour, continuous electrocardiogram, you'd find that everyone experiences a few extra heartbeats and a few skipped heartbeats. Technically, all these extra and skipped heartbeats are cardiac arrhythmias, but for most people these minor irregularities carry absolutely no health consequences. More severe cardiac arrhythmias, however, can be deadly.

Understanding your heart's electric company

What does electricity have to do with the causes of arrhythmia? Everything. In the final analysis, all cardiac rhythm problems relate to the underlying electrical activity that drives the heart and tells it when to beat and to the interaction between this electrical activity and the heart's anatomy. But before getting into what causes these electrical problems, reviewing and expanding your understanding of the heart's electric company is necessary.

As I discuss in Chapter 2, the cardiac electrical system is an exquisite grouping of cells and fibers that uses electrical impulses to tell the heart when to contract. You can follow the route of these electrical impulses, using the drawing of this system in Figure 3-1. (Don't worry; it's much easier to follow than the wiring schematic in your car manual.)

A small group of cells high up in the right atrium controls the rhythm of the heart. This group of cells is called the *sinus node,* or *sinoatrial node.* Acting as the heart's pacemaker, these cells spontaneously discharge an electrical impulse that is carried through the atrium and down to another node located at the intersection of the atria and the ventricles. Not surprisingly, this second node is called the *atrioventricular node,* or *AV node.*

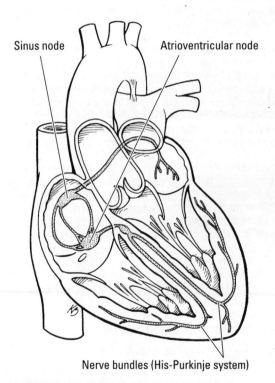

Sinus node · Atrioventricular node

Nerve bundles (His-Purkinje system)

Figure 3-1: The heart's electrical system.

Behaving like a traffic cop, the AV node receives electrical signals from the sinus node, slows them down, and makes sure that the proper number of signals alerts the ventricles to contract.

Below the AV node are two more specialized bundles of muscle fibers located in the *septum,* the muscular wall that separates the two ventricles. These specialized bundles function as pathways carrying electrical signals to contract to all of the cells in both ventricles. (If you've just got to know, these pathways are called the *His-Purkinje system.*)

Whenever this primary electrical system has problems, the heart actually has an emergency backup system. If the sinus node doesn't fire, other cells in the electrical system, such as the AV node or the His-Purkinje system can send a spontaneous signal to the heart muscle cells to contract. But there's a catch. At each lower level of command, the rate of the electrical impulse slows, so the heart beats or contracts more and more slowly.

In addition to its own internal electrical system, the heart also is influenced by the body's ultimate electrical system — the brain and central nervous system. You might say that the cardiac electrical system is *networked,* to use a modern concept. Working at its best, this network creates the ultimate flexibility for changes in cardiac rhythm that respond to the heart's particular needs. The central nervous system, for example, orders the heart to speed up when you start to run and to slow down when you rest or sleep.

When the heart's electric company goes haywire

When anything disturbs or interrupts the normal functioning of the heart's electrical system, problems with cardiac rhythm result. A variety of underlying conditions, which often are interrelated, can cause cardiac rhythm problems. These include

✔ Problems related to the electrical system itself.

✔ Lack of blood flow to living tissues of the electrical system, such as that produced by coronary artery disease (CAD), including heart attack.

✔ *Congenital abnormalities,* problems that people are born with, such as certain valve abnormalities, abnormal heart chambers, extra electrical connections in the heart that produce fast heart rhythms, or calcium growth around electrical system cells.

✔ The effect of underlying disease states or conditions, such as CAD, coronary valve disease or heart failure, stress, or even the flu.

✔ The results of things you do to yourself, such as using caffeine, tobacco, alcohol, diet pills, cough and cold medicines, or illegal drugs such as cocaine and amphetamines.

Recognizing the symptoms of cardiac arrhythmias

The symptoms of cardiac rhythm problems are as diverse as the problems themselves. They also range from inconsequential to life-threatening.

✔ **Palpitations:** Probably the least worrisome of symptoms, *palpitations* describe a variety of uncomfortable sensations of your heartbeat, such as the sensation that your heart is missing or skipping a beat.

- ✔ **A racing or pounding heart:** Although these symptoms can arise from strong emotion or exercise, if they occur while you're at rest, they may indicate a significant rhythm problem.

- ✔ **Lightheadedness or dizziness:** Everybody becomes lightheaded or dizzy every now and then, but if these symptoms are not one-time passing events, you need to have your doctor check out possible causes, which include heart rhythm problems.

- ✔ **Passing out:** Anyone who experiences a *sudden* fainting spell, or more than one episode of what seems to be an ordinary fainting spell, needs to seek medical attention to determine the underlying problem.

- ✔ **Cardiac collapse:** This most severe rhythm problem in some instances can be treated effectively with cardiopulmonary resuscitation (CPR) or automated external defibrillation (AED). Cardiac collapse (also called cardiac arrest) is without a doubt a life-threatening emergency: Approximately 95 percent of the people who suffer sudden cardiac arrest die before they reach the hospital. Quick use of CPR and AED can double their chances of survival.

Considering Heart Failure

Heart failure occurs when the heart no longer adequately pumps blood to the lungs and throughout the body. It usually is a slow process that takes place during a period of years. Underlying conditions, such as coronary artery disease (CAD), leakage from one of the heart valves, or various diseases of the heart muscle itself, usually cause heart failure. The heart initially compensates for small decreases in its ability to pump by doing the following:

✔ Enlarging *(dilatation)* to enable more blood into its pumping chambers

✔ Thickening the muscle walls *(hypertrophy)* to strengthen the pump and enable it to exert more force during its contraction to move more blood

✔ Beating faster to make up for decreased volume or power (like trying to pitch more, but smaller, pails of water on a fire)

The heart may try to compensate in these ways for years before you notice any symptoms. But when these mechanisms ultimately fail, significant heart failure occurs. By then, compensatory mechanisms often have become part of the problem.

How serious heart failure is depends on how much pumping capacity the heart has lost. A normal heart discharges about 75 percent of the blood in the main pumping chambers with each contraction, or beat. Heart failure often occurs when the amount of blood ejected per beat, called the *ejection fraction,* drops below 50 percent and when the ejection fraction falls below 40 percent heart failure ensues. Even so, many people can survive for many years with ejection fractions of only 20 percent to 30 percent, or sometimes even 15 percent.

However, the greater the loss of pumping capacity, the more likely you are to suffer a number of complications. All forms of heart failure are serious health problems that require medical treatment. Taking care of yourself, seeing your physician regularly, and paying scrupulous attention to recommended treatments are important steps you can take to improve your chances of living longer. Fortunately, significant advances have occurred during the last five years in the medical profession's knowledge of heart failure and in the treatments that are available.

Heart failure is not just one disease; it's actually a way of describing a group of conditions and symptoms that occur when any of a number of problems prevents the heart from pumping enough blood. Therefore, you can look at heart failure in several ways. The most common (described in the following list) are which side of the heart is most affected and which part of the cardiac cycle is most affected.

- **Left heart failure:** When the left ventricle of the heart cannot adequately pump blood out to the body, the blood begins to back up into the lungs. In this form of heart failure, which usually is called *congestive heart failure,* fluid seeps out of the backed-up blood vessels and into the small airways of the lungs, making them congested (hence the name). Shortness of breath is the most pronounced symptom of this condition. Several underlying conditions, which I discuss in the sections that follow, can contribute to left heart failure.

- **Right heart failure:** In right heart failure, the right ventricle isn't pumping adequately. The most obvious symptom is a buildup of fluid in the legs and ankles, a condition of swelling called *edema.* Right heart failure usually occurs as an ultimate result of left heart failure. However, people with severe lung disease can also experience right heart failure, because the right heart isn't able to generate enough pressure to pump blood through a diseased pair of lungs. This last condition is called *cor pulmonale* (see Chapter 4).

- **Systolic heart failure:** In this condition, the heart doesn't eject enough blood during its contraction, or its *systole.* Symptoms of systolic heart failure typically include lung congestion and swelling (or edema) in the legs.

✔ **Diastolic heart failure:** In this condition, the heart doesn't relax between contractions, or its *diastole*. As a result, not enough blood can enter the pumping chamber, which in turn causes fluid to gather (edema) in the abdomen and legs, a symptom that's typical of diastolic heart failure.

Defining Stroke

A stroke occurs when a blood clot or bleeding suddenly interrupts the flow of blood to an area of the brain. When deprived of blood, brain cells lose their ability to function and, if deprived for too long, die. Because brain cells and groups of brain cells have highly specialized functions, the location of stroke damage determines what loss of neurological and bodily function occurs as a result of stroke. Impairment may be temporary or permanent.

Strokes are categorized in two basic ways: ischemic stroke and hemorrhagic stroke. The causes and results of stroke depend on how and where the stroke occurs.

Ischemic stroke

An ischemic stroke occurs when a blood clot or other particle blocks a blood vessel in the brain and cuts off the blood supply to the portion of the brain supplied by that vessel. Without adequate oxygen, that portion of the brain suffers damage or even dies, resulting in such typical stroke symptoms as paralysis or problems with speech, vision, or comprehension, depending on which portion of the brain is damaged. This type of stroke is called an *ischemic stroke* because it's caused by *ischemia,* the medical term for lack of blood flow. About 70 percent to 80 percent of all strokes are ischemic, and they occur in two basic forms.

- ✔ **Cerebral thrombosis:** This form of stroke results from progressive narrowing of arteries in the brain or sometimes in the carotid arteries in the neck.

- ✔ **Cerebral embolism:** This form of stroke occurs when a blood clot, or *embolus,* travels from somewhere else in the body to the brain. When the blood clot lodges in a vessel in the brain, it cuts off blood flow to the portion of the brain supplied by that vessel.

Hemorrhagic stroke

A hemorrhagic stroke occurs when a blood vessel in or on the brain bursts and bleeds into the brain or into the space between the brain and skull. This type of stroke is called a hemorrhagic stroke because it's caused by a *hemorrhage* (in Greek, *hemo* means "blood" and *rhage* means "to break").

The brain is very sensitive to bleeding and pressure, which damage brain tissue, often permanently. Bleeding also irritates brain tissue, which swells to resist the expanding fluid. When contained, the blood forms a mass called a *hematoma;* it, too, exerts damaging pressure on brain tissue. Hemorrhagic strokes account for only about 20 percent of all strokes, but they usually are more severe and more often fatal than ischemic stroke. The two basic types of hemorrhagic stroke are

- ✔ **Cerebral hemorrhage or intracerebral hemorrhage (ICH):** This form of stroke occurs when an artery inside the brain ruptures and bleeds directly into the brain tissue surrounding the defective artery. Stress from chronic high blood pressure appears to play a primary role in damaging or weakening these small artery walls.

✔ **Subarachnoid hemorrhage (SAH):** This form of stroke occurs when a blood vessel on the surface of the brain bursts and bleeds into the cavity between the skull and the brain. Blood filling this space pushes against the brain. In very severe bleeds, the pressure on the brain from blood pushing it against the skull can cause fatal damage.

This kind of bleeding typically results from congenital abnormalities such as *aneurysms,* which are weak spots on artery walls that can balloon out, or *arteriovenous malformations* (AVM), in which a brain artery attaches directly to a vein, bypassing any capillaries. A head injury also may cause this type of bleeding.

Five tips for lowering your risk of stroke

Prevention is the most important treatment against stroke. The development of more effective treatment of hypertension during the last 20 years, for example, has lowered the prevalence of stroke in the U.S. — and that's a major breakthrough. Following these lifestyle practices will help you lower your risk of stroke:

✔ Treating high blood pressure

✔ Quitting smoking

✔ Managing heart disease

✔ Controlling diabetes

✔ Seeking help for transient ischemic attacks (TIAs)

Chapter 4

Investigating Other Cardiac Conditions

. . . .

In This Chapter

▶ Explaining peripheral vascular disease

▶ Defining valve trouble

▶ Understanding cardiomyopathy

▶ Identifying congenital heart problems affecting adults

. . . .

*I*n this chapter, I look at a variety of conditions in which the heart plays a major role — but usually not the only role. In a sense, this chapter is a kind of grab bag of heart problems. Although each condition covered in this chapter affects fewer Americans than coronary artery disease and its major risk factors, these conditions are hardly minor — particularly when you or a family member has one. Plus, most of these conditions also have links to coronary heart disease. So, buckle your seat belts for a quick tour of other important cardiac conditions.

Understanding Peripheral Vascular Disease

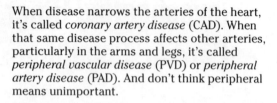 When disease narrows the arteries of the heart, it's called *coronary artery disease* (CAD). When that same disease process affects other arteries, particularly in the arms and legs, it's called *peripheral vascular disease* (PVD) or *peripheral artery disease* (PAD). And don't think peripheral means unimportant.

The narrowing of arteries in the body's extremities happens the same way it does in the coronary arteries. Fatty plaques composed of cholesterol, other lipids, and proteins build up on the artery walls to produce atherosclerosis. This condition affects about 12 percent of people ages 65 to 70 and 20 percent of those older than 70, or a total of about 10 million Americans. PVD is particularly common in cigarette smokers, and it's more common in men than in women. The most common arteries involved are those of the legs.

Although many people with peripheral vascular disease never experience symptoms, the most common symptom is pain in the leg muscles during exertion such as fast walking or climbing a hill or stairs. In medicine, this leg discomfort is called *claudication.* This discomfort or pain usually goes away when you're at rest *(intermittent claudication),* but if the arteries are totally or nearly blocked, the pain can persist even while you're resting. Severe blockage can lead to severe complications, such as leg ulcers and, rarely, tissue death requiring amputation. Having PVD also puts you at higher risk of heart attack and stroke.

Examining Valvular Heart Disease

As I discuss in Chapter 2, the four heart valves serve as traffic cops of the heart, directing blood flow in the proper direction and preventing it from improperly backing up.

As long as these valves open fully and shut tightly, all is well. But if any disease or injury causes valve leakage *(regurgitation)* or narrowing *(stenosis),* major problems can result. Significant valve leakage can overload the heart because extra blood flowing back into the heart requires an extrastrong beat to eject it. A narrowed valve can cause the heart to thicken because it is being asked to pump against a much higher pressure.

Identifying common valve malfunctions and their causes

Regurgitation and stenosis are the two most common valve malfunctions, or conditions that cause malfunctions. Although either condition can affect any or all valves, the mitral and aortic valves in the left heart, the main pumping chamber, are the ones usually affected. Both conditions can, and often do, exist simultaneously in either the same valve or different valves. A number of different conditions cause valves to leak or narrow, including:

- ✔ Congenital valvular problems (a condition you're born with).

- ✔ Damage to valve structures, such as when the structures that anchor the flaps of the mitral valve break.

✔ Progressive problems, including those that may result from the aging process, such as calcification, or those that result from an infection, such as rheumatic fever or endocarditis. If the problem becomes too severe, it may require open-heart surgery and valve replacement.

A couple of specific conditions need an extra word:

✔ **Mitral valve prolapse:** This condition is a ballooning backward of the mitral valve when the heart contracts. During physical examination, it produces a murmur and "click" heard through the stethoscope. This condition is particularly common in adolescents and young adults, especially women. Six percent to 10 percent of young women have mitral valve prolapse. (For reasons that are totally unclear, thin, young women are most often affected.)

In any event, knowing whether you have mitral valve prolapse is important because this condition makes you more susceptible to infections of the heart valve. Such infections can damage the valve enough to require surgical replacement.

✔ **Infectious endocarditis:** Heart valves can be infected with bacteria that have been introduced into the bloodstream in various ways. This condition is called *infectious endocarditis*. Although normal heart valves may contract endocarditis, it's much more common in hearts that have an underlying valve problem. Bacteria spilling into the bloodstream from dental work is a common cause of endocarditis. An infection elsewhere in the body may also cause bacteria to enter the bloodstream. Unfortunately, no symptoms specific to endocarditis enable you to identify it, but the possibility of contracting it is another reason to visit the doctor whenever you experience a persistent fever or other symptoms of infection such as night sweats, chills, or loss of appetite.

Although these infections of the heart valve can become very serious, they usually can be effectively treated with intravenous antibiotics lasting anywhere from two to six weeks. However, in some instances, the infection can become so destructive that one or more valves may need to be replaced.

The best advice: If you know that you have mitral valve prolapse with regurgitation (leakage) or any underlying valve abnormality, make sure that you take antibiotics, both prior to and after undergoing any medical procedure that might allow bacteria to enter the bloodstream — even if it's "only" a dental procedure or minor surgery. Ask your physician if you need to take antibiotics in these circumstances and which antibiotics are right for you.

Diagnosing valve problems

Because valve problems produce broad rather than specific symptoms, your physician will use your symptoms and a physical exam — in particular, a close listen to your heart with a stethoscope — when considering whether your problem may be valvular. The doctor may order further tests as necessary, including a chest X-ray and an echocardiogram, the latter of which provides images of your heart valves in action. Additionally, an MRI can produce a three-dimensional image of the valves and heart.

Treating valve problems

If a valve abnormality is not progressing rapidly or causing any serious problem, your physician may simply keep a close eye on it so that treatment can be initiated when and if it becomes necessary. Following a heart-healthy diet and lifestyle can also support valve health. Taking preventive antibiotics as needed when you have an underlying valve abnormality is a good idea.

Various nonsurgical and surgical techniques like the ones in the list that follows may be performed to correct valve problems.

- ✔ Balloon catheter procedures *(balloon valvuloplasty)* can be used in certain situations to widen a narrowed valve.

- ✔ Surgical modification and repair can be used to correct other valve problems.

- ✔ Valve replacement with either a pig's valve (porcine valve) or mechanical valve offers very effective treatment when a diseased valve cannot be repaired. Because blood clots may form on foreign surfaces of any mechanical valve, people who have these replacements must take anticoagulants for as long as they have the mechanical valve, usually the rest of their lives. Porcine valves rarely require anticoagulants, but they typically don't last as long as mechanical valves and must be replaced more often.

Understanding Diseases of the Aorta

Think of the aorta as the major superhighway leading out of the heart. For every organ in the body, including the heart, blood must first flow into and through the aorta before being efficiently distributed to all of the working tissues. (See Figure 4-1.)

A healthy aorta can take the pounding of being right next to the heart and the regular thrusts of large volumes of blood being ejected into it with each heart beat. However, various conditions can cause the aorta to malfunction. *Catastrophic* doesn't begin to describe what that means.

Identifying the causes of aorta problems

The most common problems of the aorta arise from the same disease process that affects the coronary arteries, mainly atherosclerosis.

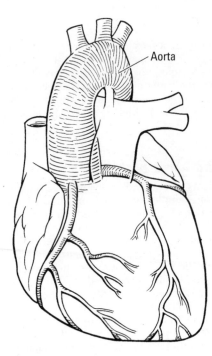

Figure 4-1: The heart and the aorta.

When the aorta becomes hardened from atherosclerosis, it can leak or even break apart, a condition called an *aortic dissection*. Aortic dissection may also be triggered by high blood pressure, pregnancy (presumably because the aorta is weakened by the extra estrogen floating around the body), or in certain abnormalities of the connective tissue. One such connective tissue abnormality is a usually hereditary condition called Marfan's syndrome, which is characterized by elongated bones, looseness in the joints and fragmentation of connective fibers in the wall of the aorta — among other things. A number of professional athletes have actually died from aortic dissections caused by Marfan's.

Aneurysms, or weaknesses in the artery wall that cause it to balloon out, also occur in the aorta. Although these aneurysms can occur adjacent to the heart, they more commonly occur in the section of the aorta that travels down the middle of the body. In this latter case, the problem is called an *abdominal aortic aneurysm* (AAA).

Diagnosing aorta problems

Aortic problems rarely produce symptoms. An aortic dissection, for example, usually occurs suddenly without warning. Detecting an aortic aneurysm earlier is possible and more common. Your doctor often can feel an aortic aneurysm by placing his or her hands on the abdomen. Because developing aneurysms exhibit no symptoms, the potential for experiencing one is another reason for having regular thorough physical exams. After you're diagnosed with an aneurysm, it needs to be carefully examined because as it continues to expand, an aneurysm can actually rupture, which results in a catastrophic outcome, usually death. Additional tests that are typically used to diagnose aorta problems are a basic chest X-ray, echocardiogram, MRI, abdominal ultrasound, and CT scan.

Treating aorta conditions

A leaking aorta is a medical emergency. A rup-
tured aorta is frequently fatal. An aorta that
leaks or is in danger of rupturing requires
surgery to replace the weakened section with a
woven Dacron graft. This surgery needs to be
performed by a highly skilled surgeon who is
familiar with this delicate procedure because
the potential for problems with coronary arteries, in addition to the aorta, is very high.

Understanding Pericarditis

Normally the *pericardium,* the thin sac surrounding
the heart, is lubricated with bodily fluids, enabling
the heart to move freely as it contracts and relaxes.
When the pericardium becomes inflamed or infected,
a condition called *pericarditis,* it can threaten rather
than protect the health of your heart.

Identifying the causes of pericarditis

A number of conditions can cause pericarditis,
including bacterial or viral infections, inflammation,
diseases of the connective tissue, and even cancer.
In a sense, many of these conditions are a result of
the pericardium serving as the last defense against
invasion of the heart; however, when these conditions occur, they can cause the pericardium to
malfunction. Your heart's ability to function can
be impeded by fluid that builds up in the pericardial
sac or fibrous tissue that infiltrates the pericardial
sac after an infection.

Individuals with pericarditis often have chest discomfort when they breathe deeply or when they lie down.
Pain when swallowing, coughing, and fever also can

accompany pericarditis. A buildup of excess fluid also can occur between the pericardium and the heart, a condition called *pericardial effusion*.

Diagnosing pericarditis

Your symptoms are the first signs leading your physician to look for pericarditis. A stethoscope exam may reveal rubbing sounds typical of fluid around the heart. An echocardiogram is one of the best tests for confirming fluid buildup around the heart and the diagnosis of pericarditis. Your physician also may order other imaging studies like chest X-rays, CT scans, or MRIs.

Treating pericarditis

Treating pericarditis requires treating the underlying condition. If pericarditis is caused by a bacterial infection, antibiotics and draining the effusion away from the heart — through a needle *(pericardiocentesis)* or through surgery — are typical therapies for resolving the pericarditis. On rare occasions, the pericardium must be removed surgically, but you can get along well without it. Pericarditis often gets better with treatment using a nonsteroid anti-inflammatory drug (NSAID) such as ibuprofen.

Understanding Diseases of the Heart Muscle

Certain conditions called cardiomyopathies can actually harm the heart muscle. About 50,000 Americans suffer from a form of cardiomyopathy. And these conditions are the leading reason for heart transplants.

Identifying types and causes of cardiomyopathies

The term *cardiomyopathy* literally means "disease of the heart muscle" (*cardio* = heart; *myo* = muscle; *pathy* = disease), and doctors speak of *cardiomyopathies* because the term covers a number of conditions. These conditions typically are classified according to the three basic effects that they have on the heart muscle and its function. Each type of cardiomyopathy may have many different causes.

✔ **Congestive cardiomyopathy:** In this type, the heart becomes *dilated,* or enlarged, and heart muscle loses its ability to contract well. A virus often causes this type of damage, but other conditions that can also cause congestive cardiomyopathy include damage from chronic, excessive alcohol consumption. In many cases, the cause is *idiopathic,* or unidentified.

✔ **Hypertrophic cardiomyopathy:** In this type, the heart muscle thickens, or becomes *hypertrophied.* Although the heart continues to contract well, the thickening of the muscle makes the pumping chamber smaller and keeps the heart muscle from relaxing properly between contractions. Hypertrophic cardiomyopathy is an inherited condition in more than half of the cases. Heart valve disease and high blood pressure are risk factors that can lead to this condition.

✔ **Restrictive cardiomyopathy:** In this type, which is rare in the United States, abnormal tissue may be deposited or grow within the heart muscle itself, causing the muscle to become stiff. This problem can occur when radiation is administered to the chest (for example, to treat a tumor elsewhere in the chest) or in certain connective tissue diseases.

Diagnosing cardiomyopathies

The warning signs of possible cardiomyopathy are shortness of breath, bloating, fainting, and chest pain. If you experience these symptoms, your physician will perform or order tests to confirm or rule out cardiomyopathy. For example, a chest X-ray can show whether the heart is enlarged. An echocardiogram can reveal heart size and muscle damage. An electrocardiogram (ECG) also can provide information about the condition of the heart's pumping chambers. Various imaging tests such as echocardiogram, heart catheterization, and nuclear stress test, may provide information on the heart's pumping ability.

Treating cardiomyopathies

The therapy for cardiomyopathies depends on the underlying condition and the type of cardiomyopathy. If an infection causes it, treatment of the infection is very important. In addition, other medicinal and surgical treatments may be employed to help the heart contract properly. In most cases, the goal of the treatment regimen is reducing the symptoms and enhancing the heart's function because, in most cases, changes to the heart muscle cannot be reversed.

Understanding Pulmonary Embolism and Deep Vein Thrombosis (DVT)

A blood clot that travels into the lungs is called a *pulmonary embolus.* Unfortunately, more than a half million Americans experience episodes of blood clots entering their lungs every year, and about 200,000 of these people die as a result. In many cases the clot in the lung arises from *deep vein thrombosis* (DVT).

Identifying the causes of pulmonary embolism

Pulmonary embolism, a clot that travels to an artery in the lungs and blocks it, typically is the result of an underlying disease. For example, people with certain types of cancer may have blood that is particularly likely to clot and cause pulmonary blood clots to the lungs. Pulmonary embolisms also are a danger for people who experience a condition called *deep vein thrombosis,* where a clot forms in a vessel in the legs or pelvis, which can result from prolonged bed rest or inactivity. Other risk factors include certain medications (such as birth control pills) and inherited clotting disorders.

The two major sources of pulmonary embolisms are

✔ Blood clots that form in the pelvic veins and deep veins of the legs — DVT. These clots, by far the most common type, break loose and travel into the right side of the heart. They are then ejected into the lung circulation where they can block blood flow to a portion of the lung.

✔ Blood clots that in some instances can actually form in the right side of the heart itself, particularly in patients with atrial fibrillation.

Diagnosing pulmonary embolism

Because a pulmonary embolism can be life-threatening, diagnosing and treating the condition as quickly as possible is important. Shortness of breath, pain associated with breathing, and sudden onset of wheezing can be symptoms. Certainly any sudden or rapidly developing shortness of breath should send you right to the doctor or emergency room. Unfortunately, this condition produces no symptoms (or only vague symptoms) in many cases, particularly when circulating blood clots are very small. The most specific tests used to confirm pulmonary embolism are spiral CT scan and *nuclear V/Q scan,* which provides images of the blood flow *(perfusion)* to the lungs. Your physician or medical-care team typically uses a range of tests to rule out other conditions that may have symptoms similar to pulmonary embolism.

Treating pulmonary embolism

Anticoagulants (blood thinners) are the most common treatment for a blood clot to the lungs. This regimen often begins with intravenous drugs such as Heparin followed by three to six months of anticoagulation with medicines that are taken by mouth. When blood clots are particularly dangerous or recurrent, a mechanical filter may also be placed in the veins coming out of the legs to actually catch the blood clots before they reach the heart and lungs.

People who have had one episode of deep vein thrombosis or pulmonary embolism are at elevated risk for repeat episodes. If you're one of those people, your physician may recommend preventive treatments, including medications, lifestyle modifications, and wearing support hose.

Understanding Cor Pulmonale

When the right side of the heart fails because of conditions in the lungs (not the heart), it's called (in Latin, natch) *cor pulmonale* (*cor* = heart; *pulmonale* = lungs).

In cor pulmonale, disorders of the lungs, such as emphysema, cause pressures to rise in the blood circulation in the lungs. This pressure in turn causes the right side of the heart to fail in its job of pumping blood into the lungs.

Treating the underlying disorder is, by far, the most effective way to deal with cor pulmonale. Certainly, stopping cigarette smoking or other irritants to the lung is very important. In addition, individuals may benefit from blood-thinning medicines to prevent blood clots from traveling to the lungs. Occasionally, lung transplant surgery is required to correct underlying lung problems that cause the right side of the heart to fail.

Understanding Congenital Heart Disease

Congenital heart disease in adults is quite rare. Congenital heart disease in newborns complicates about 1 percent of births. Treatment of various congenital abnormalities is in the domain of the pediatric cardiologist and the pediatric cardiac surgeon. When an adult patient is diagnosed with congenital heart disease, the defect probably escaped detection in childhood. Why? The defect may have been very subtle, misdiagnosed as a benign condition, or the result of inadequate medical attention. As treatment of congenital heart disease has progressed, however, more people with congenital heart disease are reaching adulthood. A team approach between pediatric and adult cardiologists benefits these patients as they grow from youth to adulthood.

More than 90 percent of adults with congenital heart disease have one of these five conditions.

- ✔ **Atrial septal defect (ASD):** An abnormal opening or hole in the septum between the two atria

- ✔ **Ventricular septal defect (VSD):** An abnormal opening or hole in the septum between the two ventricles

- ✔ **Pulmonic stenosis (PS):** A narrowing of the valve leading from the right side of the heart into the lungs

- ✔ **Patent ductus arteriosus (PDA):** An abnormal connection from the aorta to the pulmonary artery

- ✔ **Coarctation of the aorta (COARC):** A narrowing of the aorta occurring beyond the aortic valve

The treatment of congenital conditions typically requires surgical correction of the underlying defect. Atrial septal defects, however, may now be closed with less-invasive catheter-based therapies. Occasionally, medicines may be used, either as a transitional phase to support patients until they're ready for surgery or as part of the overall therapy.

Understanding Cardiac Tumors

Like any other organ, the heart is susceptible to various tumor growths. Fortunately, these *cardiac tumors* are quite rare. Unfortunately, when the heart is involved with a tumor, it is three times more likely to be a metastatic tumor that has spread from another organ system than a tumor of the heart itself. Most tumors that metastasize to the heart are close anatomically. These include lung cancers, in particular, and cancers that travel in the bloodstream (breast cancer, melanoma, and leukemia). Major tumors of the heart muscle itself are quite rare.

When the tumor is metastatic, treatment of the underlying primary cancer usually is the best course of action. Tumors of the heart muscle itself are treated with chemotherapy, radiation, and/or occasionally surgery.

Understanding Cardiac Trauma

Just like any other organ in the body, the heart can be injured in various traumatic ways, including penetrating or nonpenetrating chest injuries. The most common type of cardiac trauma occurs in an automobile accident when the chest slams against the steering wheel (another good reason to wear your seat belt). In some instances, cardiac trauma may be overlooked because other types of trauma may be more obvious. Because the ribs and muscles inside the chest cavity strongly defend the heart, it is relatively well protected. However, serious cardiac trauma can be fatal.

If the heart actually is penetrated (in medicine this is called a *laceration*), blood can leak into the pericardium, rapidly causing death. Suspecting and then checking for cardiac trauma is important anytime an individual has been in a setting where it can occur, such as a motor-vehicle accident. Recognition and rapid diagnosis of the injury through techniques such as echocardiography may prove to be lifesaving.

Surgery typically is required whenever significant cardiac trauma occurs. When you're in an automobile accident in which your chest hits the steering wheel, physicians and patients alike need to be alert to the possibility that cardiac trauma has occurred.

Finding More Information

For additional information about these and other diseases of the heart, the Web site of the American Heart Association (www.americanheart.org) offers an easy-to-use reference guide, "Heart and Stroke Encyclopedia." Other helpful Web sites include the National Heart, Lung, and Blood Institute (www.nhlbi.nih.gov), the Mayo Clinic (www.mayohealth.org), and Johns Hopkins Health Information (www.intelihealth.com).

Chapter 5

Treating Heart Disease with Nonsurgical Options

....

In This Chapter

▶ Understanding emergency CPR and defibrillation

▶ Taking an overview of lifestyle modifications that promote heart health

▶ Reviewing common drugs therapies for treating various heart conditions

....

*I*f you've been diagnosed with any form of heart disease, your physician has at his or her disposal a wide variety of treatment options. Depending upon the type and severity of your heart problem and any coexisting medical conditions you may have, these options range from simple lifestyle modifications and drug therapy to complex surgery. In this chapter, I provide an overview of the medical, lifestyle, and drug treatment options that don't require surgery or other invasive procedures (which I discuss next in Chapter 6).

Saving Lives with Emergency Medical Procedures

Two common emergency procedures that are used when you experience a sudden stoppage of the heart or rhythm problems are cardiopulmonary resuscitation and defibrillation. For people with heart disease, these emergency treatments can be lifesavers, but for many who have undiagnosed heart disease, these emergency procedures may be the first treatment they receive. The latter is a double-edged sword — fortunate because CPR and defibrillation save lives, yet unfortunate because knowing when you have cardiac risk factors (see Chapter 1) and getting early diagnosis of heart disease lead to better outcomes.

Cardiopulmonary resuscitation (CPR)

Cardiopulmonary resuscitation, commonly called CPR, is required when you experience sudden heart stoppage. CPR techniques were introduced approximately 25 to 30 years ago and have evolved since then.

The two main branches of CPR are

✔ Basic cardiac life support (BCLS).

✔ Advanced cardiac life support (ACLS).

Although ACLS requires training in skills and equipment found in an ambulance or hospital setting, virtually anyone can discover how to administer BCLS. Studies show that BCLS procedures can be lifesaving.

If a family member has serious heart disease, you need to learn the **ABCs** of CPR:

✔ Establishing an adequate **airway**

✔ Helping the individual **breathe**

✔ Establishing **circulation** by putting pressure on the chest

Courses in BCLS techniques are available in virtually every major metropolitan area in the United States. You can obtain information from the American Red Cross, a local branch of The American Heart Association, or your local health-care institution. Prompt administration of BCLS can be lifesaving. I strongly urge you to learn these techniques.

Defibrillation

Everyone who's ever watched a doctor show on TV has seen the defibrillation equipment's paddles whipped out and applied to some poor soul on the gurney. What screenwriter or director can resist such drama? And in truth, regardless of how exaggerated the TV scenarios actually are, something pretty dramatic is going on in the heart of anyone who needs the emergency procedure known as *defibrillation*.

The heart depends on a system of electrical impulses to maintain its rhythm and contract properly. Nothing good happens when this electrical system goes awry. At worst, rather than contracting, the heart simply quivers, or *fibrillates*. Because a heart that's experiencing ventricular fibrillation generates no blood flow and quickly leads to death, emergency action is required. Using those paddles you're so familiar with and an adjustable source of electricity, an electrical current is directed to the heart in an attempt to jump-start it.

After CPR, the American Heart Association rates access to early defibrillation as vital to the chances of survival for a victim of sudden cardiac arrest (sudden ventricular fibrillation). The continuing development and increased availability of *automated external defibrillators* (AEDs), which weigh only a few pounds, use long-lasting batteries, and can be operated by lay people with some basic training (such as firefighters, police, flight attendants, safety officers, sports trainers) are daily proving the value of this lifesaving procedure.

Making Positive Lifestyle Modifications

Thousands of research studies have proved that taking certain positive steps in your daily lifestyle not only lower your risk of developing heart disease but also provide powerful treatment options to help you effectively manage coronary artery disease (CAD). Appropriate lifestyle modifications, often in combination with appropriate drug therapy, may prevent or lessen the need for invasive, complicated cardiovascular procedures. I've advocated this approach to good health, which I like to call lifestyle medicine, for a long time.

Lifestyle medicine is about those daily habits and practices that clearly are proven to lower your risk of heart disease. These measures help put you in control of your life, giving you that feeling of autonomy that so many people with heart disease desire.

Following a sound nutrition plan

Eating a diet that follows heart-healthy guidelines can help you fight and even reverse heart disease and control contributing risk factors such as high cholesterol and other lipid levels, high blood pressure, and emerging markers of CAD, such as homocysteine or C-reactive protein. Such a diet is rich in fruits, vegetables, whole grains, and fiber; low in saturated fat; and just right in calories to maintain a healthy weight. The best plan also is full of pleasures and conveniences. Chapter 7 presents simple guidelines to help you achieve these goals.

Maintaining a healthy weight

Being even 10 or 15 pounds more than your optimal weight can put you at greater risk of developing heart disease and such contributing and coexisting conditions as high blood pressure, high cholesterol levels, and diabetes. Chapter 7 provides tips and techniques for helping you lose weight and maintain a healthy weight by using a sound nutrition plan.

Getting regular physical activity

Being a couch potato isn't healthy for you or the couch (chronic spring and upholstery fatigue syndrome, don't you know). For most people who have heart disease, accumulating regular, moderate physical activity as directed by their physicians can improve blood pressure, cholesterol levels, and heart function, and can combat atherosclerosis. Regular physical activity also provides crucial support for maintaining a healthy weight. Chapter 7 discusses the essential elements of a heart-healthy physical activity plan.

Reducing stress using the power of mind/body connections

A growing body of research identifies stress as one of the factors that contribute to the injury and inflammation of the coronary arteries that trigger the beginnings of heart disease and contribute to its continued progression. Stress also exacerbates the problems of heart disease in other ways. Fortunately, using simple mind/body techniques such as visualization, relaxation, biofeedback, and other natural methods of stress reduction can clearly lower your risk of heart disease.

Taking an Overview of Drug Therapies

 Thanks to extensive, ongoing pharmacological research, physicians have a wide, ever-growing array of drugs to treat the various manifestations of heart disease and the many health conditions (high blood pressure and high cholesterol included) that contribute to heart disease.

As I discuss in Chapter 3, the contributing risk factors and conditions for heart disease rarely occur singly. Most people with heart disease have a combination of contributing conditions or associated problems that require physicians to draw from a number of drugs to create an optimal treatment plan. For that reason, you may want to be able to review the major categories of drugs used in treating various manifestations of heart disease.

Use the following quick reference (which lists drug types in alphabetical order) to find out more.

✓ **Antiarrhythmics:** Approximately 30 to 40 medications are in four classes that your doctor can use to treat specific arrhythmias. For example, various medicines exist to help slow or increase heartbeat or to stabilize heart rhythm. Specific problems and some individuals may require complex combinations of antiarrhymthmic drugs, which may also need to work in concert with other heart medications.

✓ **Antibiotics:** Bacterial infections related to the heart and cardiovascular system, such as endocarditis, bacterial pericarditis, or rheumatic fever, require treatment with appropriate antibiotics. Individuals with heart valve conditions or replacements often must take antibiotics before dental work to protect them against bacterial infection.

✓ **Anticoagulants (blood thinners):** These drugs aid in preventing and treating the formation of blood clots associated with coronary artery disease and other manifestations of cardiovascular disease where clots may be a problem, such as heart attack, atrial fibrillation, stroke, peripheral vascular disease, deep vein thrombosis, or valve problems. Your doctor closely monitors your use of anticoagulants for the effectiveness of the dosage and potential problems with excessive bleeding.

✓ **Antidepressants:** Moderate to severe depression often occurs after you experience a heart attack or other severe heart event. In these cases, the physician may prescribe an appropriate antidepressant.

✓ **Anti-inflammatories:** Anti-inflammatory drugs such as aspirin (see "Aspirin" later in this list) may be prescribed to help prevent or slow the development of CAD. Other anti-inflammatories are useful for the treatment of certain heart conditions such as pericarditis (see Chapter 3).

✔ **Antiplatelets (platelet receptor inhibitors):**
Antiplatelet medicines block the ability of
platelets to contribute to clot formation. They
often are used in conjunction with aspirin and/
or anticoagulants, and some of them are given
intravenously. Your physician may prescribe
them as part of prevention or treatment for
unstable angina, heart attack, stroke, or pulmonary embolism.

✔ **Aspirin:** One of the oldest medicines in the phar-
macopoeia, aspirin still is one of the best and
truly is a wonder drug. Because it makes platelets
less sticky, aspirin clearly has been shown to
lower the risk of subsequent cardiac problems for
people who have underlying CAD. Doctors typically prescribe aspirin (81 to 350 mg daily) as a
preventive treatment for atherosclerosis, heart
attack, and stroke. Because enteric-coated aspirin
appears safer to the gastrointestinal tract, cardiologists often prescribe it for individuals who need
to take aspirin every day.

✔ **Beta blockers:** These drugs work through the
sympathetic nervous system (see Chapter 2) to
slow heart rate, decrease the force with which
the heart pumps, and help the arteries relax
(dilate). For these reasons, beta blockers are a
primary treatment for high blood pressure. They
are also useful in the treatment of stable angina
and certain arrhythmias and may be valuable in
treating heart failure in certain people.

✔ **Bile acid sequestrants:** Bile acid is produced
when your body metabolizes cholesterol. These
medicines help lower levels of blood cholesterol
by combining with cholesterol-containing bile
acid in the intestines and thus eliminating it
from the body. They're particularly useful in
lowering LDL cholesterol (the bad guys).

- ✔ **Digitalis (digoxin):** Because this drug increases the force of heart contractions but also slows the heart rate, it is useful in treating such disorders as heart failure and certain arrhythmias, particularly atrial fibrillation.

- ✔ **Diuretics:** Sometimes called "water pills," these medicines reduce fluid outside the cells in the body, passing the fluid through the kidneys and evacuating it as urine. Recent research confirms that diuretics are among the most effective and economical treatments for high blood pressure. Diuretics also are useful in treating the edema (swelling) associated with heart failure.

- ✔ **Fibric acids:** These drugs, also called *fibrates*, lower triglycerides and help raise HDL cholesterol (the good guys).

- ✔ **Inotropes:** These intravenous medicines are given to increase the heart's pumping ability. They're useful in heart failure and certain cardiomyopathies.

- ✔ **Nicotinic acid (niacin):** This medicine, a form of B vitamin, is effective in lowering triglycerides and total cholesterol while raising HDL cholesterol. Some individuals, however, find the itching and skin-flushing side effects it often produces difficult to tolerate.

- ✔ **Nitrates (nitroglycerin):** These medicines are a type of vasodilator (see "Vasodilators," later in this list) that relaxes the smooth muscles in the blood vessels and heart, lowering pressure on blood vessel walls and increasing blood flow. They're useful for preventing and relieving the chest pain of angina and for treating heart failure. They also may be used as part of the treatment in acute heart attack.

- ✔ **Statins:** These drugs, which are known as HMG-CoA reductase inhibitors, help lower cholesterol by blocking a substance used by the liver to produce cholesterol. Because they've proved so effective, statins typically are the first-choice drug therapy for reducing cholesterol levels.

✔ **Vasodilators:** These medicines relax the blood vessels, lessening pressure on the vessel walls and allowing greater blood flow. As a consequence, they are a primary treatment for high blood pressure and are useful for treating heart failure and other conditions. Three major vasodilators are ACE inhibitors, angiotensin receptor blockers (ARBs), and calcium antagonists, which are also called calcium channel blockers.

Chapter 6

Looking Into Invasive and Surgical Procedures

. . . .

In This Chapter

▶ Using electrophysiology to treat rhythm problems

▶ Opening blocked arteries with percutaneous coronary interventions

▶ Exploring several types of heart bypass surgery

▶ Understanding heart valve surgery

▶ Checking out other types of surgery

. . . .

*A*lthough many people with heart disease manage their conditions with lifestyle modifications and drug therapy, many other problems ranging from blocked coronary arteries to heart valve failures require minimally invasive medical procedures or surgery to restore higher heart function and quality of life for the patient. In this chapter, I discuss medical and surgical procedures commonly used to treat rhythm problems, atherosclerotic narrowing and blockage of coronary arteries, and heart valve problems.

Treating Rhythm Problems

Because the complex electrical impulses that control the heart's rhythm and contraction are so critical, a whole branch of cardiology has grown to detect rhythm abnormalities and correct underlying electrical problems in the heart. Here are the most commonly used medical or surgical electrical procedures involving the heart:

- ✔ **Cardioversion:** This procedure applies a small amount of electrical current to the heart, using the same equipment that is used for defibrillation. Although the procedure is not invasive, for clarity I've grouped it with the rest of treatments for your heart's electric company.

- ✔ **Automatic implantable cardiac defibrillators (ICD):** Tiny defibrillators about the size of a pacemaker can be implanted in the chest wall. The device monitors heart rhythms and automatically delivers an appropriate shock as necessary to restore proper rhythms.

- ✔ **Pacemakers:** These devices are used, either temporarily or permanently, to speed up a heart that is beating too slowly, a condition called *bradycardia*. Pacemakers actually *pace* the heartbeat by delivering electrical impulses that are very similar to the heart's own electrical system. The typical pacemaker employed now has one electrical beat that goes into the atrium and one that goes into the ventricle. These *A-V pacemakers* are powered by batteries that can last for many years.

- ✔ **Cardiac electrophysiology:** Specialized electrical catheters are placed into various portions of the heart, where monitoring or corrective electrical work can be performed either to diagnose or correct rhythm problems or other electrical abnormalities.

For example, to treat chronic tachycardia in carefully selected patients, the electrophysiologist may perform a procedure known as *ablation,* in which heat from catheter-delivered radio frequency energy is used precisely to destroy the tiny, selected parts of the heart's electrical system that are causing the tachycardia. Because they're so specialized, electrophysiology procedures typically are performed in large hospital centers.

Understanding Percutaneous Coronary Interventions (PCIs)

When atherosclerosis (CAD) severely narrows or blocks any of the major coronary arteries, threatening to cause a heart attack, *percutaneous coronary interventions* or *PCIs* often are used to relieve the problem. That fancy word *percutaneous* simply means that the cardiologist performs the procedure through the skin. (Don't you love medspeak?)

Most such procedures use a catheter that is inserted into the blocked vessel. A *fluoroscope,* which delivers real-time X-ray pictures of the vessel and catheter movements to a screen, enables the cardiologist and medical-care team to view exactly what's happening.

PCIs typically take place in cardiac catheterization labs. Patient preparation and recovery are similar for most procedures. Before the procedure, patients usually receive a sedative to relax them, anticoagulants to prevent potentially dangerous blood clots forming around the catheter or instruments during the procedure, and other medications as needed. Local anesthesia numbs the area where the catheter is inserted, usually in the femoral artery in the upper thigh but sometimes in the arm.

After the procedure is finished, the patient remains in recovery until the catheter sheath is removed from the insertion site and there's no chance of bleeding or complication at that site. Patients may then either remain in hospital or go home the same day, depending on the individual patient's condition, the nature of the procedure, and the technique used for ensuring that the catheter insertion site in the artery won't bleed. If you need one of the following PCI procedures, your doctor gives you complete instructions.

Opening blocked arteries with coronary angioplasty

Coronary angioplasty, also called *balloon angioplasty,* is a minimally invasive procedure that can quickly restore or improve blood flow through blocked arteries in patients for whom the procedure is appropriate. More than a half million patients benefit from angioplasty every year. Its formal name, which you may hear from your cardiologist or find in patient information, is *percutaneous transluminal coronary angioplasty* (PTCA).

Using the technique of heart catheterization, the cardiologist moves a specialized catheter equipped with a high-pressure balloon (on its tip) into the narrowed or blocked coronary artery or arteries. Once the catheter enters the narrowed section of the artery, the balloon is inflated. The inflated balloon stretches the artery and literally squashes the plaque up against the side of the blood vessel (see Figure 6-1). This procedure opens up the artery, enabling greater blood flow.

One drawback of conventional angioplasty is that in 25 percent to 40 percent of cases, the narrowing recurs in the artery, an event called *restenosis.* When that happens, another angioplasty, often including the insertion of a *stent* (a device that supports the expanded wall of the blood artery), or even bypass surgery may be necessary.

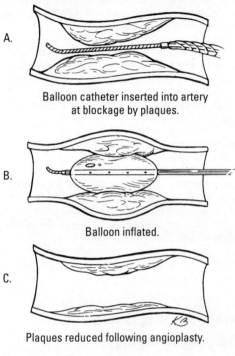

A.

Balloon catheter inserted into artery
at blockage by plaques.

B.

Balloon inflated.

C.

Plaques reduced following angioplasty.

Figure 6-1: Balloon angioplasty.

Holding arteries open with coronary stenting

In certain cases of narrowed coronary arteries in
which the narrowing process appears likely to recur,
the cardiologist may place a device called a stent in
the area where the angioplasty has occurred. These
mechanical devices look a little like coiled springs
and are designed to hold blood vessels open. Stenting

may take place during the first angioplasty to prevent recurrence of the narrowing or during a second angio-plasty to reopen the narrowing.

Stents significantly lessen the chance that the narrow-ing will recur, but they don't completely prevent it. Using specialized stents called *drug-eluting stents,* which incorporate a time-release drug, can provide additional protection against renarrowing for some patients.

Another new technique that cardiologists may con-sider using for individuals who have experienced a renarrowing or blockage of a stented artery is *coro-nary brachytherapy.* This procedure uses a catheter placed inside the artery to deliver a small dose of beta or gamma radiation directly to the artery lining where the blockage is located. Although the proce-dure appears beneficial in the short-term, the long-term effectiveness of the procedure and the long-term effect of the radiation are not yet known because the procedure still is so new.

Removing blockages with coronary atherectomy

Coronary atherectomy may be the procedure of choice when the fatty plaque blocking the artery is very hard. In this procedure, a catheter tipped with a tiny metal cone equipped with cutting edges is used to shave away the plaque from the artery walls in a process similar to Roto-Rootering. (One more reason why invasive cardiologists are called plumbers.) The loosened plaque particles then are sucked through holes in the catheter tip and removed from the blood vessel.

Removing blockages with laser angioplasty

Laser angioplasty is similar to an atherectomy in that it also removes the plaque narrowing the artery. In this procedure a laser on the end of the catheter is used to incinerate the fatty plaque deposits.

Using angioplasty immediately after a heart attack

In certain cases immediately after an individual has had a heart attack and where the conditions are appropriate, the cardiologist may use one of the forms of angioplasty I've just discussed to remove the clot (thrombus) that caused the heart attack and/or to widen the blocked artery. The objective is restoring blood flow to the damaged part of the heart muscle as quickly as possible and thus preserving as much function as possible. This procedure can be life-saving in some cases.

Looking at Coronary Bypass Surgery

Certain problems with severely blocked arteries may require coronary bypass surgery. In addition to conventional *coronary artery bypass grafting* (CABG — often pronounced "cabbage" in the lingo of physicians), recent research has developed several types of less invasive coronary bypass surgery that, although still in the experimental stage, nevertheless appear to offer equally effective results and shorter recovery times for selected individuals.

Such surgery is performed by cardiac surgeons, who train first as general surgeons and then specialize in cardiac surgery. Although they belong to different specialties, cardiologists and cardiac surgeons work closely together. Here's a look at the "gold standard" CABG and new less-invasive bypass surgical procedures.

Understanding coronary artery bypass grafting

In coronary artery bypass grafting, a piece of vein from the leg or artery from the chest is used to bypass the blockage in a coronary artery and restore blood flow.

In the conventional form of CABG, an incision is made through the breastbone (sternum) and the chest is opened to reach the heart (hence the term *open heart surgery*). At the same time, a donor vein for the bypass graft is surgically removed (*harvested,* a surgeon would say) from the leg.

In most cases, the patient also is placed on a heart-lung machine (or pump oxygenator) that takes over for the heart, which then is stopped for the surgery. The surgeon attaches one end of the bypass vein to the aorta and the other end to the blocked coronary artery below the blockage (or *occlusion*), as shown in Figure 6-2.

When all the grafts to be performed are complete, the patient is removed from the heart-lung machine, and the heart is restarted. The breastbone is rejoined using surgical wires that remain permanently in place after stabilizing the breastbone and aiding in its healing. After the surgery is complete, CABG patients are carefully monitored in the Intensive Cardiac Care Unit (ICCU).

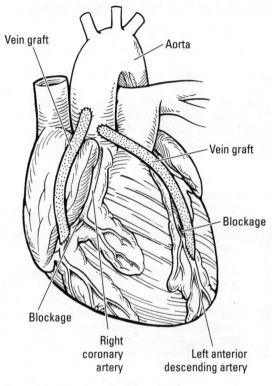

Vein graft

Aorta

Vein graft

Blockage

Blockage

Right
coronary
artery

Left anterior
descending artery

Figure 6-2: Heart bypass with two grafts.

Instead of or in addition to using donor veins for the
bypass, the surgeon may use a mammary artery from
the chest. In this case, just one end of the graft artery
is brought over and attached to the coronary artery
below the blockage, and blood then flows from the
mammary artery to the coronary artery.

Bypassing blocked coronary arteries with less-invasive surgery

Conventional bypass surgery is major surgery. It's about as *major* as surgery can get. The breastbone must be split, the heart stopped, and the patient's life supported by a heart-lung machine for several hours. This surgery has a highly successful track record, but its risks and complexity offer potential for complications for many patients. Full recovery also takes about three to six months for most patients. As a result, cardiac surgeons and specialists constantly are working to develop surgical techniques that are less difficult and less risky but still produce quality outcomes for patients.

Currently, three promising, less-invasive procedures are being used in selected, appropriate cases. They are

✔ **Minimally Invasive Direct Coronary Artery Bypass (MIDCAB):** Unlike conventional CABG, in which the breastbone is split to open the chest and provide access to the heart, in MIDCAB, the cardiac surgeon works with special instruments through a small keyhole incision in the chest wall that's about 2.5 inches to 4 inches (6 cm to 10 cm) across. As part of the incision, a tiny piece of costal cartilage on the front of a rib is removed to provide access.

At this time, MIDCAB is suitable only for individuals whose blockages are in the left anterior descending artery on the front of the heart and who need only one or two bypasses.

✔ **Off-Pump Coronary Artery Bypass (OPCAB):** This technique has grown quickly in popularity because of increasingly sophisticated technology that enables surgeons to stabilize a beating heart to safely perform surgery on it.

To perform OPCAB, the surgeon makes the same type and size incision through the breastbone as for conventional bypass surgery. Then, instead of placing the patient on a heart-lung machine, the surgeon uses a stabilizing device that holds still small sections of the heart where the surgeon is working while allowing the heart to keep beating. Benefits from OPCAB include decreased blood transfusions, decreased risk of stroke, and fewer problems with lungs, kidneys, and mental clarity, in addition to quicker recovery times.

✔ **Robot-Assisted Coronary Artery Bypass (RACAB):** Welcome to the 21st century! In this cutting-edge technique, surgeons don't perform surgery in the traditional "hands on" or "hands in" sense but manipulate a robotic device as they watch the surgical field on a video screen. The technique enables surgeons to perform precise, minimally invasive heart surgery.

Researchers envision a day when surgeons may be able to perform surgery without setting foot in the same room as the patient — your RACAB procedure in Phoenix could be performed by a surgeon in Toronto! At present, RACAB is available in only a few medical centers where research continues.

Exploring Heart Valve Surgery

As I discuss in Chapter 4, injury or disease may cause heart valves to malfunction in two basic ways:

✔ **Stenosis:** Constricting or narrowing so that they do not let enough blood flow through

✔ **Regurgitation:** Leaking as the result of defects that prevent them from closing properly

Manifestations of both problems may require medical or surgical repair. Severe malfunctions may require valve replacement.

Opening narrowed valves with valvuloplasty

In *percutaneous balloon valvuloplasty,* the cardiologist inserts a catheter tipped with a high-pressure balloon through a blood vessel into the heart. After positioning the balloon in the narrowed valve, the cardiologist inflates the balloon to stretch the constricted valve. The likelihood of the valve reconstricting is about 50 percent, so this procedure is used most commonly for individuals who have only mild or moderate valve narrowing or who cannot tolerate open-heart surgery.

Repairing heart valves with surgery

Both narrowed and leaking heart valves may be repaired using open-heart surgery and the heart-lung machine. In such a procedure, the surgeon cuts into the valve to surgically remodel its structures, enabling them to function properly. The restorative results of such surgery usually are long-lasting.

Current research in valve surgery is developing minimally invasive techniques and specially designed surgical instruments (some of which use fiber optics) that will lower surgical risk and reduce recovery times.

Replacing defective heart valves

When any of the four cardiac valves becomes so damaged that it cannot function properly and cannot be repaired surgically, the damaged valve needs to be replaced with one of the following types of *prosthetic* valves.

✔ **Mechanical valves,** which are constructed from metal and/or other synthetic materials

✔ **Natural valves,** which make use of human or animal tissue, namely valves from a pig or cow, valves shaped from the patient's own tissue, or human valves from a cadaver donor.

Each of these different valves has particular advantages and disadvantages. Surgeons always discuss the pros and cons of each type of valve with their patients. As in coronary artery bypass surgery, valve repair or replacement requires open-heart surgery and the use of a heart-lung machine.

Considering Other Forms of Cardiac Surgery

Cardiac surgeons also perform operations on other aspects of the heart, including many of the conditions that I discuss in Chapter 4. In addition, cardiac surgeons may perform surgery on other structures in the chest, including removing cardiac tumors, repairing congenital heart disease, and performing various pieces of surgery on the lungs.

Chapter 7

Living Well with Heart Disease

....

In This Chapter

▶ Recognizing that "you are what you eat"

▶ Incorporating a heart-healthy diet into your daily life

▶ Finding out why it's time to get off the couch

▶ Looking at the benefits of walking

▶ Stressing the importance of stress reduction

....

*H*ere's your chance to explore the reality that you can live well with heart disease by using a number of strategies to prevent, control, and sometimes reverse it. In this chapter, I share the basic principles, strategies, and tips that you need to work with your physician to adopt nutritional practices, a physical activity plan, and stress reduction strategies that will help you fight heart disease.

Nutrition Is Not a Four-Letter Word

Make no mistake, what you eat affects your health. The Surgeon General's Report on Nutrition and Health reminds everyone that eight of the ten leading causes of death in the United States have a nutrition or alcohol component. And heading the list as the number-one killer is cardiovascular disease — that's heart disease in simpler terms. In fact, overconsumption of dietary fat and calories and the inevitable results of added body fat are two major factors contributing to the continuing epidemic of heart disease in the United States.

Whatever trouble people eat themselves into, they generally can eat themselves out of! Even though poor food choices, such as eating too much dietary fat, contribute to significant health problems, including heart disease, adopting some simple, common-sense approaches to modifying your food choices for the better can lower your risk of heart disease and help you manage almost all heart conditions. These same smart choices also can help you control weight problems and improve health, happiness, and quality of life. These choices won't, however, bring back a good five-cent cup of coffee or improve the return on your IRA. You can't have everything.

Choosing Healthy Pleasures

Here's the first rule of heart-healthy eating: You can eat well in ways that improve your cardiac health without being a food cop.

Choose a variety of fruits and vegetables daily

Fruits and vegetables are loaded with fiber, antioxidants, and other phytochemicals that lower the risks of heart disease and cancer. In addition, because they are low in sodium and most have no fat, fruits and vegetables don't increase blood cholesterol. Studies also show that people with high blood pressure who consume a diet containing high levels of fruits and vegetables and low-fat dairy products significantly reduced their blood pressure. Last, but hardly least, fruits and vegetables are a major source of the complex carbohydrates that are the body's primary source of fuel. For these reasons, every major, responsible nutritional organization recommends that people consume a minimum of five servings of fruits and vegetables per day.

Choose a variety of whole-grain foods daily

Whole-grain products, such as cereals, breads, rice, and even pasta, form the mainstay of heart-healthy eating along with fruits and vegetables, because they are very high in fiber and in complex carbohydrates. Not consuming enough fiber clearly is associated with increased risk of heart disease. Everyone should be consuming approximately 25 grams of fiber from natural dietary sources every day, and yet the sad truth is that most folks eat only about half of this amount.

A tremendous amount of misinformation has reflected poorly on carbohydrates in the diet during the last few years. Many so-called experts have blamed carbohydrate consumption for the increased incidence of obesity in the United States Nothing could be further from the truth. *Overconsumption of calories,* coupled with

inadequate physical activity, has led to the explosion of
obesity in the U.S. Unfortunately, many of those extra
calories have come from sugars or refined simple carbohydrates, which essentially are *empty calories,* or
calories that don't provide the nutritional punch of
whole-grain products. So think *whole-grain!*

Choose healthy fats in moderation

Eating too much fat, particularly saturated fat (including transfat), contributes to two significant health
problems: elevated cholesterol and obesity, which
furthermore have clear links to increased risk of heart
disease. A high-fat diet also is linked to diabetes and
colon cancer. Moreover, eating a lot of fat, which has
nine calories per gram, compared with only four
calories per gram for carbohydrates and protein,
contributes to the overconsumption of calories by
most Americans.

For these reasons, you need to set a goal of limit-
ing the total amount of fat in your diet to less
than 30 percent of total calories and, in particular, lowering the amount of saturated fat in your
diet to less than 10 percent of total calories.
Saturated fat needs to be restricted because it
contributes directly to elevating blood cholesterol and developing atherosclerosis, which often
is called *hardening of the arteries* (see Chapter 3).

The three basic types of fat are

   ✔ **Saturated fat,** which typically comes from
     animal sources, although some fats from plants,
     such as cocoa butter, palm oil, and coconut oil
     also are saturated. Saturated fats typically are
     solid at room temperature. *Transfat,* which is
     hydrogenated or partially hydrogenated veg-
     etable oil, also is saturated fat.

✔ **Monounsaturated fat,** which comes from vegetable sources, such as olive, canola, and peanut oils, and typically is liquid at room temperature. Substantial evidence suggests that monounsaturated fats can significantly lower your risk of heart disease by raising HDL cholesterol without raising total cholesterol.

✔ **Polyunsaturated fat,** which also comes primarily from vegetable sources and typically is liquid at room temperature. Corn oil and most other salad oils are examples of polyunsaturated oils. Unsaturated fats, however, can be turned into solid forms, and thus into a form of saturated fat known as transfat, through the process of *hydrogenation.* As a result of this process, many vegetable shortenings and stick margarines are high in saturated fat, even though the manufacturing process may have started with a polyunsaturated and/or monounsaturated oil.

Use less salt and choose prepared foods with less salt

Although the American Heart Association recommends that adults consume daily less than 6 grams of salt (sodium chloride), or about 2,400 milligrams of sodium, the average adult in the United States consumes more than twice that much — 12 to 16 grams of salt per day (approximately 5 to 7 grams of sodium). That means the average person consumes about 2 or 3 teaspoons of salt daily rather than the recommended 1 teaspoon. Now, I know you don't sprinkle that much salt over your food at the table, but many prepared and convenience foods have high levels of sodium — take a glance at the labels. The same goes for restaurant offerings whether they're fast food or haute cuisine.

The major reason to limit salt/sodium intake has to do with its association with high blood pressure. In societies where less sodium is consumed, the incidence of high blood pressure is dramatically lower than it is in the U.S. If people with hypertension pay more attention to strict limitations on salt consumption and control their weight, many can manage blood pressure without medications.

 Cutting fat, cholesterol, and salt doesn't necessarily mean cutting flavor. Add healthy zip to your food by using salsas, chilis or hot sauces, mustards, vinegars, and herbs.

Choose beverages and foods to moderate your intake of sugars

Who doesn't like a little something sweet? Unfortunately, most Americans consume far too many *empty calories* (calories with no nutritional value) in the form of soft drinks, cookies, ice cream, candy, and other sweet treats. Think about these possible choices: One average candy bar or one half-cup serving of a premium ice cream contains about 275 to 300 calories (much of which is sugar and fat). For the same number of calories, you can eat two to three bananas, pears, or apples; or three to four peaches, apricots, or plums; an entire cantaloupe; a big wedge of watermelon; or a quart and a half of strawberries.

Go ahead and enjoy the occasional ice cream or candy, but for everyday eating, think in terms of "more is less" — more fruit (more nutrition) is less caloric intake.

If you consume alcohol, do so in moderation

From a cardiovascular point of view, alcohol consumption is a complex issue. Moderate alcohol consumption actually has been shown to lower the risk of heart attack. Yet, alcohol also is loaded with calories and may, therefore, contribute to weight gain. Furthermore, excessive alcohol consumption actually carries with it the cardiovascular risk of increasing blood pressure and acting in adverse ways on the cardiac muscle itself.

Moderate alcohol consumption generally is defined as one shot of distilled spirits or two glasses of wine or two beers on a daily basis. The most recent recommendations are no more than one alcoholic drink a day for a woman and no more than two for a man. Higher levels of alcohol consumption carry unacceptable health risks.

Don't consume more calories than you need

Obesity is a major risk factor for a variety of health consequences, but particularly for heart disease. About 75 percent of all mortality associated with obesity comes from the increased risk of heart disease. Although decreased consumption of fat calories decreases the risk of obesity, all calories from any source do count. The reason so many Americans are overweight is that they consume too many calories, period. Most Americans also get too little physical activity. Physical activity, as I discuss later in this chapter, helps you maintain lean muscle mass, burn more calories, and enhance cardiac health.

Managing your weight with heart-healthy eating

If you choose the foods you eat and preparation methods to promote heart health, you'll also be adopting practices that can help you lose weight (if you need to) and manage your weight at healthy levels for the rest of your life. An effective weight-loss plan based on the guidelines for heart-healthy nutrition also will feature a planned reduction in calories consumed and a planned increase in physical activity — the basis of any long-term weight management plan.

As you work to adopt heart-healthy nutrition and plan to lose weight, you may want to get some expert help. Your cardiologist may recommend a professional dietitian, or you may need to find one yourself.

DASHing into a heart-healthy diet

Although the *DASH Diet* was designed as part of a research study that tested the effect of dietary patterns on preventing and lowering high blood pressure, it offers an excellent approach for general heart health. DASH stands for Dietary Approaches to Stop Hypertension, an eating plan that reduces total and saturated fat intake and emphasizes fruits, vegetables, and low-fat dairy foods. It also limits your intake of sweets.

Read all about the DASH Diet on the DASH page (www.nhlbi.nih.gov/health/public/heart/hbp/dash) of the Web site of The National Heart, Lung, and Blood Institute (NHLBI), the study's sponsor. Among other resources, you can download a booklet with menus or you can obtain one by writing to the NHLBI Information Center, P.O. Box 30105, Bethesda, MD 20824-0105.

Believe it or not, anybody can call themselves a *nutritionist,* regardless of their training or expertise. For professional help in planning new ways of eating, I recommend that you consult a registered dietitian (RD). The RD after that professional's name means that he or she has earned a professional degree (or degrees) in nutrition and has successfully completed the national credentialing exam and other qualifications set by the Commission on Dietetic Registration of the American Dietetics Association (ADA). You can reach the Nationwide Nutrition Network, the ADA's referral service, at 800-366-1655.

Checking Out the Activity–Heart Health Connection

Literally hundreds of scientific and medical studies document the cardiac benefits of regular exercise. By the same token, inactivity poses a serious risk of developing heart disease. In one major summary study combining the results of 43 previous studies, scientists from the Centers for Disease Control (CDC) conclude that inactive people double their risk of heart disease when compared with active people. By CDC criteria, more than 60 percent of the adult population in the United States falls into the *inactive* category. It's time to get off the couch.

Getting regular physical activity can help you

✔ Lower your risk of heart disease.

✔ Improve your quality of life.

✔ Reduce anxiety and tension and elevate your mood.

 ✔ Improve your risk factors for other diseases
such as cancer and diabetes.

 ✔ Achieve and maintain a healthy body weight.

Physical activity has been shown to be beneficial
for people of all ages. If you reach the age of 65, you
have an 80 percent chance of reaching the age of 80!
Reducing your risk of heart disease and contributing
factors such as high cholesterol, high blood pressure,
and diabetes is important at any age, and keeping the
heart and muscles in tune is particularly important
for older individuals.

Easing on down the road —
into a great start

Recent guidelines from the Centers for Disease
Control (CDC) and the American College of Sports
Medicine (ACSM) recommend that every adult try to
accumulate at least 30 minutes of moderate-intensity
physical activity on most if not all days. Depending
upon your actual state of physical fitness and heart
health, your physician can help you determine what's
appropriate for you. But the two key concepts —
accumulating activity and *moderate intensity* — apply
to everyone.

Many people mistakenly think that exercise
needs to be painful to be beneficial. Nothing
could be farther from the truth, particularly
when you have heart disease. In fact, if exercise
is painful, it probably isn't good for anyone.
Furthermore, for heart patients, pain, particularly chest pain, typically is a warning sign that
you're exerting yourself too hard. Slow down.

If you charge into exercise, you'll wear yourself out at best and injure yourself at worst (particularly if you have a heart problem). Here are four basic ways to make sure that you stay within the *moderate* exertion zone — and stay with it.

✔ **Take the talk test.** Make sure that you can carry on a normal conversation with a companion while you're engaged in a bout of physical activity.

✔ **Check out your perceived exertion.** Pay attention to your body. Ask yourself, "Am I exerting myself at a moderate level or am I actually exerting myself at a light level or heavy level?" If you have high blood pressure, talk to your doctor about appropriate intensity levels. Individuals with high blood pressure or angina, for instance, usually need to work at light-moderate or lower-intensity levels.

✔ **Take your pulse.** Moderate exertion for a healthy individual takes place between 60 percent and 70 percent of your predicted maximum heart rate. For individuals with high blood pressure or a heart condition, moderate exertion takes place at lower percentages of maximum exertion, so ask your physician for specific instructions.

To estimate your maximum heart rate, subtract your age in years from 220 beats per minute. Thus, for a 40-year-old individual, the predicted maximum heart rate is 220 beats minus 40 beats — 180 beats per minute. The moderate exertion level of 60 percent to 70 percent of 180 beats equals 108 to 126 beats per minute.

✔ **Use a heart-rate monitor.** You can find inexpensive heart-rate monitors on the market that accurately keep track of your heartbeat during exercise and take the hassle out of accurately determining your exertion level. I particularly recommend the use of a heart-rate monitor if you have high blood pressure or any type of heart disease, or if you've experienced a heart attack.

Choosing the best activity for you

People often ask me what is the best activity or exercise to promote heart health and general fitness. My answer never changes: It is the form of exercise that you will do! Look at *all* the things you like to do, because somewhere in that list is an activity that will get you started.

Ask yourself these three questions to increase your chance of selecting the right activity program. And then answer them honestly. (No daydreams of making the next Olympic team.)

✔ What do I like to do?

✔ What is convenient for me?

✔ What have I successfully done in the past?

Every beginning exerciser needs to build his or her program around a core of what are called *aerobic* exercises. *Aerobic* literally means "in the presence of air." So aerobic exercises are those that require your muscles to burn more oxygen and you to breathe faster. Hard-working, air-hungry muscles demand more oxygen-rich blood from the heart. The heart in turn works a little harder and grows stronger. In this way, aerobic exercise helps lower the risk of heart disease. Although you work at lower levels of intensity when you already have heart disease, aerobic activity still will be the foundation of your activity program.

Many different kinds of aerobic activities and exercises exist. All of them are good for the heart. Pick the ones that you think may be most convenient for you, or, better yet, mix and match. I also need to emphasize that daily forms of physical activity, such as leaf raking, lawn work, gardening, even brisk housework, all qualify as *moderate* physical activity and all are equally beneficial for the heart. Make them part of your overall plan.

Recently, considerable attention has been paid to the health benefits of strength training. Although strength training has multiple overall benefits, it should not be the core exercise for people who want to prevent heart disease or, in particular, who already have heart disease.

Involving your physician

Preventing or managing heart disease requires teamwork. As I said earlier, let your doctor know of your desire to participate in a program of regular physical activity and seek his or her guidance. Most doctors welcome the opportunity to talk about lifestyle measures with you and can help you fine-tune your physical activity program to account for your unique personal circumstances such as current medications, current level of physical activity, and current physical conditions, including existing heart disease. You may consider having an exercise tolerance test before starting to exercise.

If you already have any heart condition, taking an exercise tolerance test prior to starting a program of physical activity is important. Talk to your physician about it. In addition, older people, people who have one or more risk factors for heart disease (see Chapter 1), and people who have been inactive also may benefit from such testing.

Developing a personal plan for physical activity

When it comes to sticking with physical activity long term, people usually falter on simple issues rather than complex issues. In addition to choosing an activity (or activities) that is enjoyable, convenient, and with which you've been successful in the past, you must remember that achieving the goal of a healthier heart through physical activity is a race that is won by the tortoise and not the hare.

Adopting the following watch words can help you plan your personal program. In fact, you may even want to post them on your mirror or tape them to your sweatband.

- ✔ Start slow.

- ✔ Progress slowly.

- ✔ Use common sense to avoid dangerous symptoms.

- ✔ When in doubt, ask your doc. (Even if you think your question is silly, the risk of embarrassment is much less harmful than going down with a heart attack or, worse yet, sudden death.)

If you've previously been inactive, starting out at a low level of moderate intensity, such as walking five minutes per day, represents a good beginning. After you're comfortable with that level of exertion, you can increase it slowly. Try building up your walk or other activity by approximately one minute per week until you reach 30 minutes on most, if not all, days.

Of course, don't leave your common sense at home! If you have any symptoms such as chest discomfort during a walk, you need to slow down or stop and discuss the symptom at the earliest possible time with your doctor. Remember that the most important heart benefits from regular physical activity accrue to individuals who find ways of remaining physically active throughout their lives.

Symptoms to watch for during exercise

The key to safe exercise is never leaving your common sense at home. Staying in tune with any symptoms that you have during an exercise session is important for achieving maximum benefit and safety from exercising, especially when you're at risk for heart disease or already have established signs or symptoms or manifestations of heart disease.

If the following symptoms occur during exercise, *contact your physician* before continuing any form of physical activity.

✔ **Discomfort in the chest, arm, upper body, neck, or jaw:** This type of discomfort may be angina and may be of any intensity and may be experienced as aching, burning, or a sensation of fullness or tightness. Discuss it with your physician.

✔ **Faintness or lightheadedness:** These symptoms may occur after exercise whenever your cool-down is too brief. This situation usually isn't serious and can be managed by extending the cool-down. However, if you experience a fainting spell or feel that you're about to faint during exercise, immediately discontinue the activity and consult your physician.

✔ **Excessive shortness of breath:** You can expect the rate and depth of your breathing to increase during physical activity, but you shouldn't feel uncomfortable. A good rule to follow is that breathing should not be so difficult that talking becomes an effort. If wheezing develops or if recovery from shortness of breath takes more than five minutes at the conclusion of an exercise session, you need to consult your doctor.

✔ **Irregular pulse:** If your pulse is irregular, skips, or races, either during or after exercise, such that it differs from your normal pulse, consulting your physician is important.

✔ **Changes in usual symptoms:** If your usual symptoms change — an increase in angina or shortness of breath, for example — or pain occurs or becomes more severe or persistent in an arthritic joint or at the site of a previous orthopedic injury, you need to consult with your physician.

✔ **Any other symptoms:** Finally, you always need to discuss any other symptoms that concern you with your physician. Pain is a warning sign that you should never ignore.

Some medications can also affect the intensity of your exercise program but not its effectiveness. Discuss this possibility with your doctor.

Walking Your Way to a Healthier Heart

Patients often ask me what exercise I recommend for heart health. My enthusiastic answer never changes — walking! Yes, walking — that simple skill you've been competent in since you were a year old. Most people, however, underestimate the power of regular fitness walking.

Extensive research conducted by my laboratory and others demonstrates some simple facts about walking.

✔ Virtually everyone can get aerobic benefit from walking. Walking is particularly suitable for patients with a variety of heart conditions because the intensity is extremely flexible.

✔ Walking is usually the simplest and most convenient form of physical activity for the vast majority of people.

✔ Walking is simple — as easy as putting one foot in front of the other, opening your front door, and setting off down the road.

✔ Most of the research that shows that regular physical activity lowers the risk of heart disease has focused on walking.

✔ For most people, I recommend walking as the best form of regular exercise to lower the risk of cardiovascular disease — and so do 90 percent of my fellow physicians.

If you prefer a different form of physical activity and/or aerobic exercise, however, don't be dismayed. Almost everything I say about walking also applies to other forms of aerobic exercise. All aerobic activities are equally good in terms of their cardiovascular benefits.

Understanding the Connections between Stress and the Heart

High stress levels constitute one of the cardiac health risks (and general health risks) that everyone faces daily. In fact, a growing body of scientific and medical evidence links stress to a variety of illnesses ranging from heart disease and cancer to the common cold. Unfortunately, stress is pervasive in today's modern, fast-paced society. One study from the National Institute of Mental Health found that more than 30 percent of adults experience enough stress in their daily lives to impair their performance at work or at home.

Despite literally hundreds of studies about stress, a precise definition is frustratingly difficult to come up with. Perhaps the best simple definition came from Canadian scientist Hans Selye, who in 1956 defined stress as "the nonspecific response of the body to any demands made on it" in his pioneering book *The Stress of Life*. The *demand* (the thing that stresses you out, be it a traffic jam, power outage, or deadline) and the *response* (your internal reaction to, say, a $1,500 car-repair bill or any other demand) are the key components of stress.

No doubt you're faced with many demands (stressors) every day. How you respond is up to you, but remember that the way you respond can contribute either to improved cardiac health or to increased cardiac risk.

Many people don't realize that having positive stress is possible. But a certain amount of stress may be necessary for you to reach your optimal performance. For example, outstanding athletes often perform at their best in the "big game." And you may be one of the many people who work best when faced with a deadline. However, when stress becomes excessive or when your response to the stress becomes negative, your health in general, and your cardiac health in particular, may be harmed.

Linking stress to heart disease

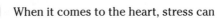

When it comes to the heart, stress can

- ✔ Increase your likelihood of developing coronary artery disease (CAD).
- ✔ Create chest discomfort that can mimic heart disease.

✔ Cause palpitations or even very serious arrhythmias.

✔ Contribute to the development of high blood pressure.

Numerous scientific studies link job-related stress to an increase in the likelihood of your developing coronary artery disease. Some of these studies show that heart attacks occur more often during the six months following negative life changes, such as divorce, financial setback, or the death of a spouse or close relative than they do during the six months before these negative life changes. Although this evidence isn't as strong as the evidence that links heart disease to other established major risk factors, such as elevated cholesterol, cigarette smoking, and physical inactivity, it nevertheless is strong enough to make stress a risk factor for heart disease.

Linking stress to high blood pressure

The link between stress and high blood pressure is well established. Many years ago, Dr. Walter Cannon, a famous physiologist, coined the phrase *fight or flight* to describe the physiological changes that occur during stress. He linked this response to the genetic makeup of humans. When confronted by a dangerous and frightening saber-toothed tiger, for example, ancient human ancestors needed to make an immediate decision whether to stand and fight, freeze with fear, or immediately take flight. One physiological response to this stress is elevated blood pressure.

Unfortunately, people still have the genetic makeup that causes their blood pressure to rise during emotionally stressful situations. For example, studies show that air-traffic controllers, whose jobs place them under continually high levels of stress, are more likely to have high blood pressure than people in many other professions.

Constant pressure caused by events and situations over which you feel you have only minimal control is a particularly dangerous form of stress. For example, blood pressure rises in soldiers during times of war, in civilians faced with natural disasters, such as floods or explosions, and in entire societies in which social order is unstable.

Linking Type A personality traits to heart problems

About 40 years ago, Dr. Ray Rosenman and Dr. Meyer Friedman developed the concept of *Type A Personality,* which links certain kinds of behavior and personality traits with an increased incidence of heart attack. Unfortunately, the concept of Type A behavior often is loosely and incorrectly applied to any hard-driving, busy worker.

The research defines Type A behavior, however, as containing aggression, competitiveness, and hostility. Individuals who exhibit true Type A behavior also are likely to have a sense of incredible urgency as they attempt to accomplish poorly defined goals in the shortest period of time. Likewise, they often are angry when confronted with unexpected delays. The combination of *frustration* and *anger* is essential to manifest the cardiac danger associated with a Type A personality.

Hard workers who are happy in their work, even when they're workaholics, are more likely to fall into what Rosenman and Friedman characterized as *Type B personalities* and are not at increased risk of heart disease.

Linking anger to dangerous heart problems

Recent studies from a variety of investigators, including Dr. Redford Williams at Duke University, show that the hostility component of Type A behavior specifically accounts for almost all the increased risk of cardiac disease. Using one of the subscales on psychological inventories administered to many participants in large heart-health trials, Dr. Williams and his colleagues identified cynical mistrust of others, frequent experience of angry feelings, and overt expression of cynicism and anger in aggressive behavior as key factors that make up the psychological profile that increases the risk of developing heart disease. In real-life situations, this discovery points not only to the knowledge that anger kills when you let it control your behavior — think road rage — but also to the knowledge that it may also kill by damaging your heart.

Keeping Stress and Anger at Bay

Do you get bent out of shape when the weather ruins your plans? When a driver cuts you off? When a last-minute project keeps you late at work? If you do, you're risking serious damage to your heart, which can stand up to only so much stress and anger. Reducing these risk factors is up to you, and it's not as hard as you may think.

Controlling stress with a four-part plan

Stress may be dangerous for the heart, but the good news is that some simple strategies may significantly lower stress and thereby improve cardiac health. Here are four ways to lower the stress in your life and contribute to cardiac health:

✔ **Modify or eliminate circumstances that contribute to stress and cardiac symptoms.**

People often simply do not realize that aspects of their daily lives can compound problems with stress. Cutting back on caffeinated beverages, such as coffee, tea, and many soft drinks, for example, may make a substantial difference in your stress levels and manifestations like cardiac palpitations. Fatigue and insomnia may also contribute to stress, so be sure that you get plenty of rest and a good night's sleep whenever you're experiencing symptoms of stress. You also need to avoid the temptation to use alcohol as a way to relax. Although it may seem to offer a temporary release from stress, it usually leads to greater problems.

✔ **Live in the present.**

The basis for all effective stress reduction is being able to live in the present. It may sound simple, but many people spend an inordinate amount of time either regretting the past or fearing the future. Strategies such as biofeedback, visualization, and medications can help you live in the present and substantially lower stress levels.

✔ **Get out of your own way.**

Many people compound the inevitable stresses of their daily lives by layering on negative feelings concerning these stresses. Recognizing that no one can live a life that is completely free of stress is as important as trying not to compound the problem by allowing feelings of negativity or low self-worth to make stress worse.

✔ **Develop a personal plan for stress.**

Developing a personal plan to alleviate stress is one of the most effective ways to handle it on an ongoing basis, instead of allowing it to become free-floating anxiety. Many people find that daily exercise, meditation, taking a timeout (either alone or with family), and other such strategies provide effective ways of controlling the stresses of daily life.

Controlling anger with five simple steps

The hostility or anger component of the Type A personality poses the most significant cardiac risk. Here are five simple strategies for helping you control anger:

✔ **Learn how to trust other people.** An open heart is a healthy heart. Individuals who are isolated and fearful of other people increase their risk of cardiac disease. By making an effort to open yourself up to trusting other individuals, you can substantially lower your risk of heart disease.

✔ **Plant a garden and care for a pet.** The Irish poet William Butler Yeats said the definition of a civilized human being is one who plants a garden and cares for a domestic pet. This concept is not only a prescription for a civilized human being, but also a prescription for a heart-healthy life.

✔ **Practice asserting yourself.** Many people keep their emotions bottled up inside. They're often pleasantly surprised to find out that by standing up for what they believe (in a pleasant way, of course), they can control unwarranted stress in their lives and lead a happier daily existence.

- ✔ **Become a volunteer.** A wonderful body of literature suggests that volunteers not only do good for other people, but they also improve their own health. Somehow, the act of giving of yourself to other people results in improved health for yourself.

- ✔ **Practice forgiveness.** Many people keep themselves in a constant state of anger for wrongs or supposed slights from other people or from the world at large. Learning how to forgive others is one of the very best things that you can do to improve your own cardiac health. While you're at it, forgive yourself, too, for past shortcomings — imagined or real.

Chapter 8

Ten Signs and Symptoms You Need to Know About

. . . .

In This Chapter

▶ Understanding which symptoms suggest heart disease

▶ Recognizing your heart's distress signals

▶ Knowing when to take symptoms to the doctor

. . . .

*A*lthough medical signs and symptoms can overlap, you can distinguish between the two on the basis of who is experiencing them. For example, you may regard a nagging, worrisome cough as a *symptom*. Your doctor, however, may regard that cough as a *sign* of congestion of the lungs.

In broad terms, then, *symptoms* are feelings or conditions that a patient experiences and then tries to describe to his or her physician. *Signs* are findings that the physician derives from the physical examination that point toward the proper cardiac diagnosis.

Depending on the circumstances and severity, some symptoms (conditions you experience) may represent signs of serious cardiac disease to your physician or may not be worrisome at all. In this chapter, I look at ten key symptoms and signs.

Chest Pain

Chest pain probably is the most common symptom for which people go to see a cardiologist. Although chest pain can signify heart problems, it also can stem from a wide variety of structures in the chest, neck, and back that have no relation (other than proximity) to the heart. The lungs, skin, muscles, spine, and portions of the gastrointestinal tract, such as the stomach, small bowel, pancreas, and gallbladder are among these structures.

Pain caused by angina or heart attack usually is located beneath the breastbone but may also be located in the front of the chest or either arm, neck, cheeks, teeth, or high in the middle of the back. Exercise, strong emotion, or stress may also provoke chest pain.

Very short bouts of pain lasting five to ten seconds typically are not angina or heart-related but are more likely to be musculoskeletal pain. If you have concern about *any* chest discomfort, going to a medical facility and having it further evaluated is imperative.

Shortness of Breath

Shortness of breath is a major cardiac symptom. But determining whether this symptom comes from problems with the heart, the lungs, or some other organ system typically is difficult.

Exertion can cause temporary shortness of breath in otherwise healthy individuals who are working or exercising strenuously or in sedentary individuals who are working even moderately. But an abnormally uncomfortable awareness of breathing or difficulty breathing can be a symptom of a medical problem. Shortness of breath that occurs when you're at rest, for example, is considered a strong cardiac symptom.

If shortness of breath lasts longer than five minutes after activity or occurs when you're at rest, have your doctor evaluate it.

Loss of Consciousness

Loss of consciousness usually results from reduced blood supply to the brain. Perhaps the most common loss of consciousness is what people usually call a *fainting episode.* This temporary condition may be brought on by being in a warm or constricted environment or in a highly emotional state. Such episodes often are preceded by dizziness and/or a sense of *fading to black.* When the heart is the cause, loss of consciousness typically occurs rapidly and without preceding events.

Cardiac conditions ranging from rhythm disturbances to mechanical problems potentially can cause fainting or a blackout. Because such cardiac problems can be serious, never dismiss the loss of consciousness in an otherwise healthy individual as a fainting episode until that person has a complete medical workup.

Cardiovascular Collapse

You can't experience a more dramatic symptom or greater emergency than *cardiovascular collapse,* also called *sudden cardiac death.* Of course, cardiovascular collapse results in a sudden loss of consciousness, but the victim typically has no pulse and stops breathing. The victim of a seizure or fainting spell, on the other hand, has a pulse and continues breathing.

Cardiovascular collapse can occur as a complication in an individual who has known heart disease but sometimes may be the first manifestation of an acute heart attack or rhythm problem.

When cardiovascular collapse occurs, resuscitation must take place within a very few minutes or death inevitably follows. Being able to respond quickly to cardiovascular collapse is the greatest reason for learning CPR or basic cardiac life support.

Palpitations

Palpitations, which can be defined as an unpleasant awareness of a rapid or forceful beating of the heart, may indicate anything from serious cardiac rhythm problems to nothing worrisome at all.

Typically, an individual who is experiencing palpitations describes a sensation of a *skipped beat;* however, people also may describe a rapid heartbeat or a sensation of lightheadedness. Whenever the palpitation is accompanied by lightheadedness or loss of consciousness, it is imperative that a further workup be undertaken to determine whether serious, underlying heart-rhythm problems are present.

Often, the simplest underlying causes of palpitations can be turned around by getting more sleep, drinking less coffee or other caffeinated beverages, decreasing alcohol consumption, or trying to reduce the amount of stress in your life. Nevertheless, you need to take this problem to your doctor for evaluation first.

Edema

Edema is an abnormal accumulation of fluid in the body, a type of swelling, and has many causes. The location and distribution of the swelling is helpful for determining what causes it. If edema occurs in the legs, it usually is characteristic of heart failure or of problems with the veins of the legs.

Edema with a cardiac origin typically is *symmetric,* which means that it involves both legs. If the edema is an abnormal gathering of fluid in the lungs, called *pulmonary edema,* the typical symptom is shortness of breath. This symptom also can be typical in a patient with heart failure.

Abnormal gathering of fluid in either the legs or the lungs always indicates the need for a complete cardiac workup to determine whether each of the heart's main pumping chambers is working adequately.

Cyanosis

Cyanosis, the bluish discoloration of the skin resulting from inadequate oxygen in the blood, is a sign and a symptom.

One form of cyanosis occurs when unoxygenated blood that normally is pumped through the right side of the heart somehow passes into the left ventricle and is pumped out to the body. This anomaly commonly occurs in congenital abnormalities that create abnormal openings between the right and left sides of the heart.

The second type of cyanosis commonly is caused by constriction of blood vessels in your limbs or peripheries and may be the result of a low output from the heart or from exposure to cold air or water. Whether the cyanosis is central or peripheral in nature guides a physician in the search for which type of underlying condition is causing the cyanosis.

Any form of cyanosis is a symptom that should prompt discussion with your physician.

Cough

As anyone who has had a head cold knows, a cough can accompany a viral illness. It can also represent a variety of underlying causes such as cancers, allergies, abnormalities of the lungs, or abnormalities of the breathing tube. The cardiovascular disorders that result in cough are those that cause abnormal accumulations of fluid in the lungs, such as significant heart failure.

Take any prolonged or unexplained cough to your doctor. Certainly whenever blood is present in what you cough up, you need to have the possible causes checked out. The same goes for any evidence of bacterial infection, typically yellowish, greenish, or blood-tinged sputum.

Hemoptysis

Coughing up blood of any kind — from small streaks in sputum to large quantities — is called *hemoptysis* in medicine. This condition can result from a variety of very serious diseases of the lungs or even some forms of cancer. Whatever the cause, coughing up blood-tinged secretions is never normal and may represent a medical emergency.

 If you ever cough up blood in any form — no matter how minor it seems — contact your doctor immediately.

Fatigue

In busy, hectic lives, *fatigue* may stem from a bewilderingly large number of underlying causes ranging from depression to side effects of drugs to physical illnesses, including cardiac problems.

The ordinary fatigue you feel after working hard is normal, even when you have to crash into bed early. But a significant level of *enduring* fatigue should always prompt a call to your doctor, who may want to do an appropriate medical workup to determine possible underlying causes.

Diet, Health & Fitness Titles from For Dummies

For Dummies books help keep you healthy and fit. Whatever
your health & fitness needs, turn to Dummies books first.

**Diabetes For Dummies,
2nd Edition**
0-7645-6820-5

**Diabetes Cookbook For Dummies,
2nd Edition**
0-7645-8450-2

Asthma For Dummies
0-7645-4233-8

Thyroid For Dummies
0-7645-5385-2

Menopause For Dummies
0-7645-5458-1

Migraines For Dummies
0-7645-5485-9

**Overcoming Anxiety
For Dummies**
0-7645-5447-6

Depression For Dummies
0-7645-3900-0

**Dieting For Dummies,
2nd Edition**
0-7645-4149-8

**Nutrition For Dummies,
3rd Edition**
0-7645-4082-3

After you've read the Pocket Edition, look for the original Dummies book on the topic. The handy Contents at a Glance below highlights the information you'll get when you purchase a copy of *Heart Disease For Dummies* – available wherever books are sold, or visit dummies.com.

Contents at a Glance